W9-BKK-418
3 1702 00101 8146

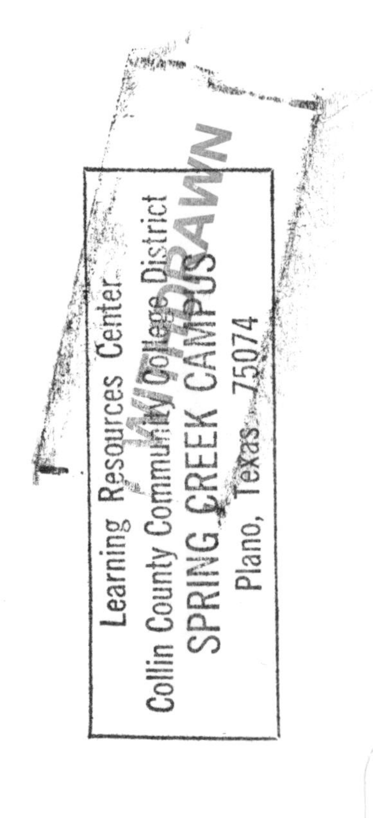
Learning Resources Center
Collin County Community College District
SPRING CREEK CAMPUS
Plano, Texas 75074
WITHDRAWN

Forecasting Elections

Michael S. Lewis-Beck
University of Iowa

Tom W. Rice
University of Vermont

A Division of Congressional Quarterly Inc.
Washington, D.C.

1414 22nd Street, N.W., Washington, D.C. 20037

Printed in the United States of America

Cover design: Paula Anderson

Library of Congress Cataloging-in-Publication Data

Lewis-Beck, Michael S.
Forecasting elections / Michael S. Lewis-Beck, Tom W. Rice.
p. cm.
Includes bibliographical references and index.
ISBN 0-87187-600-0
1. Election forecasting--United States. 2. Election forecasting--France. 3. Election forecasting. I. Rice, Tom W., 1956- . II. Title.
JK2007.L48 1992
324.973'00112--dc20 91-39418
CIP

CONTENTS

TABLES AND FIGURES

Tables

Figures

PREFACE

As political scientists we aim to *explain* politics. In addition to this goal, which we share with others in our field, we aim to *forecast* political events, specifically, election results. This is not an activity many scholars of elections pursue, which is not to say that election forecasting does not occur; indeed, it goes on all the time. Politicians, journalists, pollsters, and individual voters engage in speculation, even heated debate, about who will win the next election. In essence, all these people are making forecasts. But absent scientific rules of prediction, these forecasts are little more than guesses.

In this book, we systematically develop formulas (models, if you will) to forecast election results for the U.S. presidency, House of Representatives, Senate, governorships, and state legislatures. For comparative purposes, the more complex French electoral system also is studied.

To derive our forecasting models, we examine patterns in historical data from the post-World War II period (1948-1990). After reviewing the relevant research literature, we put forth an explanation of vote choice for each election arena. These explanations, in turn, serve as the foundations of the forecasting models. Take, for example, presidential elections. Why do voters select one candidate over another? Why George Bush and not Michael Dukakis in 1988? Research has demonstrated that economic issues were important vote determinants in 1988, just as they have been in other U.S. presidential elections. Thus, we consider the economy in our explanation of presidential election results, along with other relevant variables, such as party strength and candidate appeal. Our explanation is then summarized in an uncomplicated formula called a regression model, and the model is evaluated for its explanatory and predictive power. At every step, we offer descriptions that we hope will lead to a clear understanding of these models. Good descriptions, coupled with good data, enable readers to make good forecasts for themselves.

Many institutions and individuals contributed to the preparation of this book. We cannot mention them all, but we would especially like to thank the students in our undergraduate classes in American politics, who were the guinea pigs for much of this material. Their helpful comments and sharp criticisms brought about many improvements in the text. In particular, we wish to acknowledge John Engle, Wendy Sender, and Ellen Faustine for their valuable research assistance. The manuscript also benefited from the valuable critiques and suggestions supplied by the evaluators. Also, our copy editor, Nola Healy Lynch, did an excellent job of identifying trouble spots in the writing. We are grateful to our editorial team at Congressional Quarterly—Brenda Carter, Kerry Kern, and Jenny Philipson—for their insight and skill in producing this text, and to Paul Pressau for his typesetting expertise. We would also like to thank Tracey Bonesteel, who, courtesy of Macro International Inc., helped us prepare the graphics. We take responsibility for any errors that remain.

CHAPTER 1

Prognosticators to Pollsters: Traditional Forecasts

Forecasts fill our daily lives. Before venturing out in the morning most of us check the weather forecast, and some of us consult the horoscope page of the newspaper. Listening to the radio on the way to school or work, we hear the latest economic forecasts. At lunch our waiter suggests that we will enjoy the leek and potato soup. In the afternoon we hear a botany professor discuss the dangers of acid rain, or perhaps we hear our boss predict climbing company profits in the months ahead. Back home for the evening, we review the latest line on the big game before calling a fellow fan to make a friendly wager. And many of us finish the day the way we started it, by checking the weather forecast.

The events just described are disparate in many ways, but they all involve forecasts. The horoscope "forecasting" our day, the waiter "forecasting" our taste for a soup, and our boss "forecasting" company profits—all predict things to come. Indeed, any guess about some condition in the future is a forecast.

By this definition, elections rank among the most frequently forecasted public events. Take the 1988 presidential race, for instance. In the weeks and months before the balloting countless political observers offered their predictions on who would win. The techniques they used to generate their forecasts varied widely. A few, with tongue in cheek, relied on simple methods such as the famous World Series dictum: "If the American League wins the series, the Republican candidate will win the election." For those prognosticators 1988 was a bad year; Republican George Bush handily defeated Democrat Michael Dukakis, despite a World Series victory by the Los Angles Dodgers of the National League.

Other, more prudent, forecasters stuck to their own intuition and experience. But many of these guesses were wide of the mark as well. For example, former President Richard Nixon predicted Dukakis would defeat Bush "decisively" (Andrew Sullivan, *New Republic,* August 29, 1988, 15). And, at one point, *Washington Post* columnist Haynes Johnson detailed a state-by-state scenario for a Democratic victory (*Washington Post,* March 11, 1988). Finally, major polling firms, examining the electorate's current preferences, saw Dukakis in the lead until the waning weeks of summer.

Of course, not everyone predicted the Democrats would capture the White House. Election forecasters never speak in one voice. For each of the sages who foresaw a Dukakis victory, there were several others who thought Bush would win. Divided predictions may confuse the citizen who simply wants to know who is likely to win.

In this book, we try to make forecasting something other than so much mumbo jumbo. This is an important task, for several reasons. First, and most obviously, as citizens we are concerned about the political future of the country, namely who will govern in our democracy. Thus it is important to be able to tell good forecasting methods from bad. Second, as students of politics, we want to better explain election outcomes. As shall be seen, good explanations lead to better forecasts, and vice versa. Finally, as professional political scientists we hope to encourage the practice of macro-level forecasting, already followed in fields such as economics, where important indicators like the unemployment rate or the gross national product (GNP) are regularly forecast.

To begin, we concentrate on the distinction between nonscientific and scientific modes of election prediction. In brief, the nonscientific approaches—those of prognosticators, pundits, and politicos—are flawed in that they do not rely on carefully formulated reasons, or hypotheses, that are subjected to systematic test. By way of contrast, the scientific approaches—polling and modeling, for example—employ modern methods of sampling and statistical estimation. We elaborate on the strengths and weaknesses of these different approaches in the remainder of this chapter. Then, in subsequent chapters, we develop explanations for national election outcomes, based on leading theories of voting behavior. In testing these explanations, the basics of regression analysis are explicated. Initially, we construct a forecasting model for presidential elections. Then we move on to Congress and the American states. For purposes of comparison, we also formulate a French national elections model. Finally, we apply our models to forecasting the 1992 election outcomes, the next national elections as of this writing. Our explanation of traditional election forecasting methods begins with prognosticators.

Prognosticators

Election prognosticators, in our definition, rely on signs or rules to foretell outcomes. Usually these signs or rules have no ostensible connection to the political process. A classic example, from early Greece, is the study of animal entrails to divine who will be chosen to lead. A more contemporary example comes in the aforementioned World Series rule. Other signs used by prognosticators to prophesy who will be elected president of the United States include these:

- The Beaujolais rule: "If the Beaujolais wine harvest is poor, then the Republican will win."
- The height rule: "The taller candidate will win."
- The name rule: "The candidate with the longest last name will win."

Although such rules provide good sport, they are not to be taken seriously because their apparent predictive power is based on chance. To express this important criticism in everyday language, we say "it just so happens" that Republican success is associated with American League victories or bad Beaujolais. Or, it is "only a coincidence" that name length relates to candidate success. The laws of probability tell us that out of the millions of events that precede American presidential elections every four years, at least a few will correlate highly with the party that captures the White House.

Given the laws of probability, any of us can become prognosticators of this sort: simply identify an event that happens before presidential elections and varies systematically with the winner. With this in mind, we set out to discover some other "chance" rules. As our standard for accuracy, we decided to use the World Series rule. In the post-World War II era the rule has predicted eight of the eleven presidential contests correctly, missing only in 1988 and 1980 (when Republicans George Bush and Ronald Reagan won despite an American League loss) and in 1948 (when Democrat Harry Truman won despite a National League loss). Searching the pages of a standard reference volume, we quickly came up with the following rules:

- The mascot rule: "If the mascot of the team that wins the Rose Bowl is an animal, the Democrat will win."
- Easter Sunday rule: "If Easter falls in April, the Republican will win."
- The Academy Awards rule: "If two different pictures win at least two each of the top six awards (best actor, best actress, best supporting actor, best supporting actress, best director, and best picture), the Democrat will win."
- The Stanley Cup rule: "If Montreal or Toronto wins hockey's Stanley Cup, the Democrat will win."

Our exercise demonstrates how easy it is to find events that correlate with the party that wins the presidency. But, intriguing as these congruences are, they must be attributed to luck. Moreover, these rules, like the World Series maxim, do not always work. The mascot rule fails to forecast correctly three presidential elections (1964, 1972, 1976). The Easter rule, the Academy Awards rule, and the Stanley Cup rule break down twice each (respectively in 1960 and 1976, 1964 and 1972, 1956 and 1968). Similarly, each of the more widely known rules have erred. The Beujolais rule, dating back to 1960, did not get it right in 1988: the classically fruity wine produced by that autumn's harvest did not precede a Democratic president. The height rule accurately forecasted the Bush victory in 1988, but it missed the 1976 race (Carter versus Ford). The longest name rule was wrong in 1988, as well as in 1984. Of course, these failures are not surprising, since the rules are not based on any serious causal connection between the prognostication sign and presidential choice. These correlations are chance events and, even when nearly perfect, do not imply causation.[1]

However, the argument that prognostication rules rest on chance is not always so easy to make. Take the following rule, for example:

- The bellwether rule: "As the bellwether goes, so goes the nation."

The idea is straightforward: certain geopolitical units (usually states or counties) accurately reflect the voting preferences of the entire country. Thus, if you know how the citizens of the bellwether region plan to vote, you know how the nation as a whole will vote.[2]

The notion of bellwethers has long been part of American political lore. Perhaps the most famous bellwether is Maine. From 1860 to 1932 the state voted for the winning presidential candidate in sixteen of the nineteen elections, prompting the cry, "As Maine goes, so goes the nation!" Its special standing was threatened in 1936, however, when only Vermont joined Maine in voting Republican. Gleeful Democrats immediately coined a new bellwether aphorism, "As Maine goes, so goes Vermont!" Lamentably for Maine, the 1936 miscue proved to be the first of many. Over the 1936 to 1988 period the state voted for the winning presidential candidate in only seven of the fourteen elections.

The demise of Maine as a barometer of national preferences led many observers of elections to search for a replacement. Economist Louis Bean devoted much of his impressive scholarly life to the pursuit of the perfect bellwether. For forecasting presidential elections he favors watching the larger states, especially New York, California, and Illinois (Bean 1972, 34). More recently, C. Anthony Broh (1980) concluded that New Mexico was the state to monitor—that state, from its beginning, has gone for the presidential winner in every election but 1976. Henry Kenski and Edward Dreyer (1977) picked Delaware, citing its string of perfect predictions from 1964 through 1988. Edward Tufte (1974, 46-54), in a thorough analysis of the topic, identified three "superbellwether" counties: Crook County, Oregon; Laramie County, Wyoming; and Palo Alto County, Iowa. All three voted for the winner in every presidential contest from 1916 to 1972.

How do these bellwethers work? Consider the celebrated Palo Alto County example. By the 1980s the county's reputation as a bellwether was so well established that the national media sampled the preferences of its citizens in the weeks before the election. (There is even talk of a super-superbellwether within the county, the small Silver Lake Township.) One reason commonly offered for the predictive success of the county is that, somehow, it is a microcosm of the nation. That is, Palo Alto may be a representative sample of American voters and their attitudes and behaviors. But if that is what it takes to be a good bellwether, Palo Alto seems an unlikely candidate. The county's small, scattered population (mostly descendants of nineteenth-century Northern European settlers), live on farms or in small towns. They certainly do not represent a typical cross-section of late twentieth-century America.

Another explanation for Palo Alto's success is that the residents have special predictive qualities. That view was espoused by the editor of the county's largest newspaper, the *Emmetsburg Reporter-Democrat.* When asked to account for her county's remarkable record, she replied, "We are well-read, educated, and we care" (Lewis-Beck 1985, 53). If these are the special qualities of the citizens of Palo Alto County, they are more an informed elite than a representative sample of Americans. If that is the case, it becomes even more difficult to explain how the county's voting preferences manage to match those of the American public in election after election.

Most likely, the citizens of Palo Alto County are not a microcosm of the U.S. electorate, nor do they have special predictive qualities. What seems more probable is that their predictive success derives primarily from chance. The same judgment would apply, of course, to the citizens of Crook and Laramie counties, the citizens of New Mexico and Delaware, and the citizens of any other geopolitical unit. Given that there are more than 3,000 counties in the United States, it is not all that surprising that a few counties have voted for the winning presidential candidate every time between 1916 and 1972. Palo Alto just happened to be one of the lucky few, along with Crook and Laramie. When the number of observations (counties) gets so large, the laws of probability suggest that seemingly amazing coincidences will occur.[3]

Especially because there is no plausible causal explanation or set of reasons for the bellwether's success, the expectation is that its luck will run out. In fact, this has happened. The first of the three counties to fall was Laramie, which voted for Ford in 1976. Both Palo Alto and Crook

County survived the 1980 contest, but Palo Alto fell in 1984, when it went for Mondale. A common explanation was that Mondale grew up in a nearby Minnesota county and often visited Palo Alto. The citizens of Palo Alto appear to have been swayed by a well-documented determinant of vote choice termed "friends and neighbors" voting (see Key 1949; Lewis-Beck and Rice 1983). The implication is that vote choices in Palo Alto County, like vote choices everywhere, are subject to standard explanations of electoral behavior. In this sense, the county's citizens are no different from other Americans; they are just luckier when it comes to voting for winning presidential candidates.

At this juncture, the luckiest citizens of all remain those of Crook County; a Bush vote in 1988 preserved their string of victories. However, eventually even the citizens of Crook County will probably back a losing candidate. When that happens some new county, perhaps one that has predicted every race since 1920 or 1924, will assume center stage for a brief run as a bellwether.

Politicos

Rules for prognostication, whether based on the World Series or bellwethers, are entertaining. However, in the end they are unconvincing forecasting tools because they are mere games of chance. To make reliable election forecasts we must look less at coincidences and more at politics. That is, the political process itself must be directly examined for clues. This is something party activists do continually. Campaign workers, party regulars, officeholders, and candidates themselves constantly assess how they are doing among prospective voters. These politicos, as we will label them, frequently make their predictions public before an election. As forecasters, their great appeal is that they are political insiders. They live and breathe politics; they know the ins and outs. In preparing a forecast, they draw from experience and from a vast network of contacts. When they say So-and-So is going to win, they are often believed. Their hunches seem to make good sense. After all, they have been "on the Hill," "with the staff," or "on the campaign trail."

Here is a sampling of the predictions that politicos made about the 1984 presidential and congressional election outcomes. Consider first the presidential race. Rep. Mary Rose Oakar (D-Ohio) declared that Mondale would capture her state, underlining her conviction in a $1,000 bet with Reagan's southern campaign director, Lee Atwater (*New York Times,* October 30, 1984, 12). While campaigning in California, Mondale staffers regularly announced that their candidate was behind the president by only 8 points or so, while the Reagan people put the number at about 17 points (*New York Times,* October 28, 1984, 1, 12). Just days before the election, candidate Mondale asserted that "the Republicans are in for the biggest surprise of their life" (*New York Times,* November 5, 1984, 15). Of course, after the votes were counted, President Reagan had been reelected in a landslide. Obviously, the forecasts of these Democratic politicos, while perhaps motivated by a necessary optimism, contained considerable error.

However, at least in 1984, the error was not all on the Democratic side, as evidence from the House of Representatives contests shows. Going into the election, the House was composed of 167 Republicans, 266 Democrats, and 2 vacant seats. During the campaign, Republican leadership hammered away at the notion that the party would achieve a major victory. President Reagan forecasted that Republican House candidates would be swept into office on the coattails of his reelection in "an historic electoral realignment" (*New York Times,* November 5, 1984, 1). Trent Lott (R-Mississippi), the minority whip, boldly projected an absolute Republican majority, which would have required a net gain of about 50 seats (*Washington Post,* September 24, 1984, 4A). A bit more cautiously, the minority leader, Robert Michel (R-Illinois), speculated that there would be a Republican surge of 30 to 40 seats (*Washington Post,* September 24, 1984, 4A). In the end, Republicans picked up only 14 seats, far below the forecasts of these politicos.

What unites all these erroneous forecasts? Partisan bias. When politicos forecast they tend to favor their own candidates and party, regardless of objective conditions. As a result, they will almost invariably project a greater margin of victory (or narrower margin of defeat) than in fact occurs. Of course, this behavior is understandable. They believe—or at least want to say publically—that their party will do well. In particular, they may hope to convey a sense of confidence in order to rally the party faithful, worry the opponents, and sway the undecided. Further, many politicos rely on likeminded politicians for their information. All this makes it unlikely that politicos will openly forecast defeat. (Or, if defeat is too obvious to be denied, they will probably underestimate the extent of the losses.) In short, the partisan bias that infects politicos renders them unreliable forecasters. If a politico makes a surprisingly accurate prediction, we may well suspect, as with prognostication rules, that it was a lucky guess.

Pundits

Politicos are not the only "experts" who routinely forecast elections. Journalists, essayists, think-tank scholars, and other learned critics also speculate on election outcomes. We group these professional commentators into the category of pundits. An essential difference between pundits and politicos is that the former are freer of partisan bias. To be sure, pundits may be known to favor a certain political perspective, usually liberal (such as David Broder and Tom Wicker) or conservative (such as George Will and William F. Buckley), but they tend to have little immediate interest in the success of a particular party. Thus, arguably, they are more able to offer objective predictions.

We might, of course, expect some individual pundits to be better forecasters than others. Nevertheless, it is important to get a sense of the accuracy of pundits' predictions in general. The 1952 presidential race between Republican Dwight Eisenhower and Democrat Adlai Stevenson provides us with a good opportunity to do that. Two weeks before the balloting *Newsweek* asked fifty "of the nation's top political writers," most of them Washington, D.C., correspondents for major newspapers, who they thought would win the election (*Newsweek,* November 3, 1952, 36). Rarely have such a large number of seasoned political observers been polled at the same time. Their forecasts could not have been more divided; twenty-six picked Stevenson to win and twenty-four chose Eisenhower. So, while pundits may be "objective," objectivity can certainly lead to very different predictions. Eisenhower ended up winning the election in a landslide, picking up 55 percent of the popular vote and 442 of the 531 electoral votes. Only one of the fifty political analysts predicted that Eisenhower would win more than 400 electoral votes, and only three predicted that Sevenson would win at least 350.

In fairness to pundits as a group, they are not always so varied or so wrong in their opinions. They seem especially able to make a simple yes-no prediction of the winner when an incumbent landslide is in the offing. For example, in the *Newsweek* poll of political analysts taken two weeks before the 1956 election, forty-seven thought Eisenhower would win and only three sided with Stevenson. On election day Eisenhower swept Stevenson by an even larger margin than in 1952.

In more recent elections, when outcomes were more uncertain, pundits have fared less well. Take the critical 1986 Senate races, for instance, in which a rare Republican majority was under challenge. Right before the balloting, the *Wall Street Journal* asked a number of political observers to make predictions (see Lewis-Beck 1987, 57). One of these, Paul Weyrich, the publisher of *Political Report,* projected that the Republicans would retain control of the Senate. In opposition, Alan Baron of the *Baron Report* thought the Democrats might gain a bare majority. Pundit William Schneider forecasted a healthy Democratic majority (54 seats). When the votes were in, Schneider proved closest to the mark, as the Democrats netted 8 seats for a majority of 55 to 45. (Interestingly, while Schneider's accuracy shows how good a single pundit can be, it serves to underscore the relatively poor performance of the other pundits.)

In the 1988 presidential race, the pundits' record was also sometimes tarnished. Reflecting on the topsy-turvy prenomination campaign and the inability to predict primaries accurately, essayist Mary McGrory wrote a column entitled "Where Did We Pundits Go Wrong?" (*Washington Post,* March 13, 1988, C1). Poking fun at his own forecasting errors, David Broder titled a piece "Did I Say That?" (*Washington Post,* December 28, 1988, A19). As already noted, another *Washington Post* writer, Haynes Johnson, foresaw a Dukakis victory. Columnist George Will also warned of a potential Democratic win (*Washington Post,* March 10, 1988, A27). In contrast, M.S. Forbes, Jr., had self-assuredly predicted an easy Bush victory (*Forbes,* November 14, 1988, 25). Bush actually won with 53.4 percent of the popular vote, a comfortable, but not an easy, victory. Analyst Kevin Phillips, though, managed to get it about right; on election eve he forecasted a Bush popular vote of between 53 and 55 percent (*Wall Street Journal,* November 4, 1988, A16).

Taken as a whole, then, pundits' predictions are unreliable. Sometimes their guesses are on target, sometimes they are way off. Why do these trained political observers miss as often as they do? One possibility is that after all, like the politicos, pundits have political biases that inject error into their forecasts. Although their biases may be more subtle, they still may influence the type of information the pundits gather and how they interpret that information.

Suppose, however, that we do not care about all pundits. Instead, we have a favorite pundit, hypothetical journalist Sally Seer. Imagine that we like her political columns because they appear informed, thoughtful, and impartial. Moreover, let us say that she recently forecasted a difficult race correctly (for example, the 1986 Senate split). Should we count on her when we want another accurate election forecast? The answer is no, for two reasons: the problems of replication and repetition.

As the word suggests, *replication* concerns reproducing Ms. Seer's forecasts. That is, can we, acting independently, employ her methods to come up with the same forecast? Unfortunately, it is unlikely. Pundits' forecasts are almost always based on informal observations, conversations, and insights. By their nature, these methods are difficult to convey and even more difficult to replicate. We are forced to take their word for it because we cannot check their methods. Moreover, this concern over replication applies to the pundit herself. Can she replicate her methods? Since they are so informal, it is quite possible that she cannot. Even if she had the "formula" right the first time, it could well be lost the second time around.

If Ms. Seer is unwilling or unable to share her forecasting secrets with us, the importance of repetition becomes paramount in judging her credibility. Can she repeat her 1986 success election after election? A perfect forecaster would be right all the time. Any election forecaster worth her salt should be right most of the time. So to evaluate Ms. Seer, we should examine her track record. How many election forecasts has she ventured, and how accurate have they been?

Upon inspection, we would almost surely find that Ms. Seer called some races right and some races wrong. Her reliance on insight, informal networks, and experience to make her forecasts is simply too imprecise to render accurate predictions time and again. The shortcomings of Ms. Seer's methods are shared by all pundits. Add to this the fact that pundits may not be entirely objective and you have a recipe for mediocre forecasting.

Pundits' predictions, then, need to be viewed with some caution. In any major election campaign, many professional observers will make forecasts. A few of these pundits (perhaps your favorite) will guess correctly. But before labeling these individuals forecasting experts, see if they pass the twin tests of replication and repetition. Almost certainly, they will not.

Pollsters

The traditional methods of forecasting discussed thus far have been flawed in one or more serious ways. Prognostication rules rest on coincidence. The projections of politicos are heavily contaminated with partisan bias. Pundits have difficulty reproducing their methods and repeating their successes. Furthermore, none of the approaches is based on modern scientific techniques of research. By contrast, the systematic public opinion survey of contemporary pollsters offers a forecasting method that overcomes these limitations.

It is important to distinguish first between scientific and nonscientific election surveys. This distinction has become especially important in light of the growing number of preelection surveys. For example, according to Karlyn Keene, editor of *Public Opinion* magazine, 124 presidential election polls were released to the press from September to November of 1988 (*New York Times,* November 10, 1988, 5). In terms of election forecasting, which are more likely to be accurate? Why? We begin our discussion with a popular sort of poll that is frequently inaccurate: the straw poll.

Since the nineteenth century, newspapers have been taking straw polls of their readership. The results often make front page news. In our bellwether county of Palo Alto, the *Emmetsburg Reporter-Democrat* has held a straw poll for every presidential race since 1952. In the weeks before each election the paper publishes a ballot form that readers may fill out and return to the paper's office. In 1984, these ballots gave the nod to Ronald Reagan (at 51 percent of the 280 preferences returned).

While this forecast was right for the nation, it was wrong for Palo Alto County, as we have seen.

Straw polls are not always off the mark, however. An interesting one that proved to be correct was the 1952 "cigarette survey." Before the presidential election that year two brands of cigarettes were marketed nationwide, an "I Like Ike" brand and a "Stevenson for President" brand. Sales were tracked closely, and at election time the "Ike" brand was edging out the "Stevenson" brand, 51.8 percent to 48.2 percent (*Newsweek,* November 3, 1952, 35). As we know, Eisenhower went on to win the election.

Perhaps the most infamous straw poll was the one conducted by *Literary Digest* magazine before the 1936 presidential election. The publication mailed out ballots to owners of automobiles and telephones. Millions of people responded. The magazine tallied the ballots and splashed the results across its pages the week before the election. The headlines declared that Alf Landon would defeat Franklin Roosevelt easily. On election day Roosevelt swamped Landon, 60 percent to 37 percent. *Literary Digest* went out of business shortly thereafter. (For an excellent critique of the poll, see Squire 1988.)

Straw polls are sometimes right, sometimes wrong. The people they sample may or may not represent the voting population. That is, these polls tell us the views of those who respond; but this group may be, and often is, very different from those who actually vote. In a word, straw polls, as they are traditionally done, are not scientific (see Roll 1968).

What makes a poll scientific? Of paramount importance is the sampling methodology. If the people interviewed are not selected properly, even well-designed questions administered by professionals will not produce results we can count on. In technical terms, the correct way to choose a set of respondents is to use probability sampling methods based on principles of random selection. With a probability sample, every unit in the population under study has a known, nonzero probability of selection. Applied in an election survey, it means that every eligible voter in the electoral district has had a chance of being interviewed (and the size of that chance can be calculated). Imagine that we put the names of all the eligible voters on separate pieces of paper, toss them in a big barrel, and draw names out one by one to be interviewed. In other words, we execute the classic probability sample, a simple random sample (without replacement of the names). In that case, every name in the barrel (every eligible voter) will have an essentially equal chance of being selected. Of course, it would be impractical to carry out an election survey in exactly this way. Intuitively, though, the example is useful, for it illustrates the principles of randomness and nonzero chance of selection.

Traditional straw polls violate the rules of probability sampling. For instance, not every citizen of Palo Alto County has an opportunity to fill out the ballot published in the *Emmetsburg Reporter-Democrat* poll. Many voters in the county, such as those who do not have a copy of the paper, have no chance to participate in the survey. And, if these people think about politics differently than those who buy the paper, then the straw poll will probably misrepresent the views of the county as a whole. This is precisely what happened in the *Literary Digest* poll. The magazine mailed ballots only to people who had an automobile or a telephone. In 1936 the people with automobiles and telephones tended to be better off financially, and they tended to be Republicans. They also tended to vote for Republican Alf Landon in the straw poll. The millions of people without an automobile or a telephone tended to be Democrats. They never had the opportunity to participate in the survey and show their support for Democrat Franklin D. Roosevelt.

Probability sampling, then, is a basic principle of scientific polling (for a complete discussion of probability sampling, see Kalton 1983). In practice, reputable survey organizations, such as Gallup and Harris, rely on it to a great extent. However, they can vary in how they finally select respondents in the household for interviewing. Because of the pragmatic tradeoffs that sometimes have to be made in order to contain costs, polling organizations may use the designation "modified probability sampling."

But how accurately can polls that use some form of probability sampling forecast election outcomes? To make this question more concrete, consider the problem of forecasting the outcome of a U. S. House of Representatives race in any of the 435 districts. Suppose we are commissioned to conduct a poll one week before the election in district *X*, where incumbent Smith faces challenger Brown. Given the study budget, we can afford to select a probability sample of 1,500 likely voters (in statistical notation this sample is represented as $N = 1{,}500$). Carefully trained interviewers ask each of the respondents the following question: "In the upcoming election for the House of Representatives, whom do you intend to vote for, Smith or Brown?" The results, when tallied, show Smith with 52 percent, Brown with 48 percent, and an unlikely 0 percent undecided. (For the moment, we leave aside the problematic assumptions that for our sample we have no "undecideds" and that we have identified people who will actually vote.)

At first blush it appears that a forecast for Smith is in order. But we must remember that a typical congressional district could have 200,000 voters, and we are dealing with a sample of only 1,500. Viewed from this perspective, it might seem possible, even likely, that our results will be in error. Fortunately, statistical theory can tell us the chances that our findings are off the mark. In particular, it can be shown statistically that with a sample size of 1,500 out of a population of 200,000, we can be 95 percent confident that the percentage estimates of support for Smith and

Brown do not vary from the preferences of the district voters as a whole by more than plus or minus (±) 3 percentage points. This means that the true support for Smith among all voters is almost surely between 49 and 55 percent, and that the true support for Brown is very likely between 45 and 51 percent. (For an accessible discussion of sample sizes and error margins, see Weisberg and Bowen 1977.)

These interval forecasts (the percentage estimate, ± 3) suggest that Brown, despite being behind in our poll, could actually be ahead of Smith in the vote, 51 to 49 percent. (Compare the lower end of the range for Smith with the upper end of the range for Brown.) In light of this possibility, we would be prudent to declare the race too close to call, rather than to predict a Smith victory. That is exactly what most professional pollsters do when faced with a situation like ours in district *X*. They have learned to be wary when the interval forecasts indicate that either candidate could win.

Races too close to call can make life difficult for pollsters interested in forecasting. Unfortunately for them, such results are not that uncommon. To illustrate, let us consider how many races would likely be too close to call if the survey methodology of district *X* were applied in each of the 435 House districts. First, assume something that is essentially correct: one-fourth of House incumbents win reelection with less than 60 percent of the vote. Label these "contested races." Since approximately 90 percent of House races typically have incumbents running, that means a total of about 98 contested races. Assume, further, that each survey can expect 6 percent "undecided" voters, rather than the unrealistic 0 percent in our previous example. The large number of undecided voters, coupled with the standard sampling error of ± 3 percentage points, means that often no candidate will be confident of majority vote support in the electorate, at least in these 98 contested races. (For instance, because of the "undecideds," it would be difficult for a candidate in one of these races to register 53 percent support in a poll. But, even with a tally of 53 percent, sampling error would mean that he or she could not count on a majority among voters.) Therefore, the outcome of many these races will necessarily appear uncertain on the basis of the survey results.

Even races that appear quite safe to call sometimes turn out differently than expected, just by chance. Recall that statistical theory holds that with a sample of 1,500 we can be only 95 percent sure that a candidate's vote percentage will fall in our forecast interval. What about the other 5 percent? That 5 percent represents races—and we do not know which ones they will be ahead of time—that we might call incorrectly. Suppose in our survey a candidate polls 54 percent of the vote, producing an interval estimate of 51 to 57 percent. As a result, we call the election for the candidate. There is a 5 percent chance, however, that the candidate will win less than 51 percent or more than 57 percent of the vote on election day. If the candidate garners less than 51 percent (a 2.5 percent chance—half of the 5 percent chance), he or she may lose and our forecast will be wrong. Thus, a few of our "safe" calls will be wrong simply because probability sampling does not profess complete certainty.

Another potential problem that political pollsters face is that standard sampling error margins may not hold for election surveys. A recently completed study of election polls by William Buchanan (1986) found that many missed the mark by a margin greater than the ± 3 percentage points expected on a probability survey of 1,500 respondents. He concluded, "On the basis of the long-term performance of the polling profession as a whole, press accounts of predictions should say '5 percent margin of error' where they now say '3 percent.' " Obviously, if he is right, the number of House races that would be too close to call could exceed 100.

Why does real prediction error often surpass the error suggested by statistical theory? One reason is that a survey may be improperly conducted. Poorly trained interviewers may be used or the questions may be badly phrased. The nonrespondents may come disproportionately from a relevant subpopulation; for example, if the interviews are all conducted by telephone calls to homes in midmorning, a lot of middle-aged, working-class people will be missed. Each of these factors can lead to a sample that does not really represent the voting public and that will thus yield poor election predictions. (For a full discussion of sources of error in preelection surveys, see Crespi 1988.)

However, a major reason for error, which we have only alluded to so far, is the difficulty of sampling those who will actually vote. If estimates of voter preference are based on a sample that contains, in part, people who will not actually vote, then additional error is inevitable. Polling firms employ different methods to "validate" voters. Most election surveys begin by asking respondents how likely they are to vote in the upcoming election. The response categories differ from poll to poll, but a common range of choices looks something like this: "very likely," "somewhat likely," "not very likely," and "not at all likely." Some pollsters proceed to interview only respondents who say they are "very likely." Others include with that category those who are "somewhat likely." (A few even add those who are "not very likely.") Further, some polls also ask whether the respondent is registered to vote, and interview only from that group. (A few polls even exclude respondents who say they did not vote in the last major election.) Thus, the population of individuals "qualified" to be interviewed varies, depending on how "likely voters" are defined. No solution is foolproof; after all, even registered voters who say they plan to vote may change their minds on election day. Assessing who will turn out, then, is a critical problem for pollsters.

Table 1.1 Iowa Poll Results for the 1978 Senate Race

	Vote intention		
Poll date	Senator Clark (Democrat)	Challenger Jepsen (Republican)	Undecided
May	55%	29%	16%
July	53	31	15
September	52	40	8
November	51	41	7
Actual Vote	48	51	

Source: Data from the Iowa Poll, *Des Moines Register,* July 30, 1978, 12A; September 17, 1978, 11A; November 5, 1978, 1.

Note: The May and July results are based on "all Iowans," while the September and November results are based on "likely voters," that is, those who say they are registered and will definitely vote. The reported sampling error is ± 4 percent.

Citizens may also change their minds about whom they intend to vote for. If this change occurs after the interviewing, then the poll-based forecast will be off. A vivid example, which combines elements of both types of change—turnout and preference—comes from the 1978 Senate race in Iowa between incumbent Democrat Dick Clark and Republican Roger Jepsen. During the campaign, the preferences of Iowans were tracked regularly by the respected Iowa Poll, conducted by the state's leading newspaper, the *Des Moines Register.* Table 1.1 displays the results of the Iowa Poll over the course of the campaign. Clark had a consistent and substantial lead. Even the last survey, executed only a few days before the election, showed Clark with a comfortable 10 percentage point margin over Jepsen. On election day, however, Jepsen defeated Clark convincingly, 51.1 percent to 47.9 percent.

The failure of the Iowa Poll to predict the Jepsen victory does not appear to be due to shoddy methodology. The *Des Moines Register* has substantial experience in polling and has called numerous other races correctly. A more likely reason for the miss is that voter intentions (whether to vote and for whom) shifted to Jepsen in the final days of the race. Sifting through the extensive press accounts that followed the Clark defeat, it seems probable that the change in voter intentions came out of a very strong, eleventh-hour push by anti-abortion forces against Clark.

One practical message is that in order to monitor such last-minute shifts, pollsters may have to take surveys right up until the election. Look at the 1988 example of the New Hampshire primary, when Gallup stopped polling early and erroneously forecasted that Senator Dole would beat Vice President Bush. As a response to hazards of that sort, Jeffrey

Table 1.2 Final Preelection Poll Forecasts for the 1984 Presidential Race

Polling organization	Reagan	Mondale	Margin
USA Today	60%	35%	25%
NBC	58	34	24
New York Times/CBS	58	36	22
Gallup	59	41	18
Washington Post/ABC	54	40	14
Harris	56	44	12
Roper	55	45	10
Actual vote	59	41	18

Source: Wall Street Journal, November 8, 1984, 7.

Note: In instances where the Reagan and Mondale percentages total less than 100, the polling firm did not allocate undecided respondents.

Alderman, survey director at ABC News, said, "The first lesson I learned was that once you start polling, you don't stop" (*New York Times,* November 10, 1988, 5).

Polling close to the election does not guarantee precise forecasts, however. To illustrate, consider the "day before" presidential election polls in 1984. That year, as in every presidential year since the 1940s, many major pollsters conducted voter preference surveys during the last few days preceding the election. The results of seven of these polls are reported in Table 1.2. Not surprisingly, all the surveys correctly predicted a clear victory for Reagan over Mondale. (Reagan led in the polls throughout the campaign and defeated Mondale 59 percent to 41 percent in the election.) What is interesting from a forecasting perspective is the wide disagreement over the margin of that victory: from the 25 percentage point spread of *USA Today* to the 10 point spread of Roper. A 25 point spread would represent the largest landslide in the history of presidential elections, while a 10 point spread is a much more modest, if comfortable, victory, similar to that of Bush over Dukakis in 1988.

The differences in forecasts from these pollsters cannot be explained by the standard sampling error argument (of ± 3). Indeed, the 15 point difference from the top to the bottom prediction cannot even be accounted for by using Buchanan's (1986) previously mentioned more cautious rule (of ± 5). Instead, the differences seem attributable to the various other problems of election survey methodology. It is important for the users of polling data to be aware of the potential for such problems, in order better to evaluate a particular poll's projection.

Table 1.3 Gallup Presidential Preelection Poll Results, 1948-1988

Poll date	Election winner (loser)	Poll result for: Winning candidate	Losing candidate	Other/ undecided
Oct. 25, 1948	Truman (Dewey)	44%	50%	6%
Nov. 1, 1952	Eisenhower (Stevenson)	47	40	13
Nov. 2, 1956	Eisenhower (Stevenson)	57	39	4
Nov. 4, 1960	Kennedy (Nixon)	49	48	3
Oct. 30, 1964	Johnson (Goldwater)	64	29	7
Nov. 2, 1968	Nixon (Humphrey)	42	40	18
Nov. 4, 1972	Nixon (McGovern)	61	35	4
Oct. 30, 1976	Carter (Ford)	46	47	7
Nov. 1, 1980	Reagan (Carter)	47	44	9
Nov. 3, 1984	Reagan (Mondale)	57	39	4
Nov. 6, 1988	Bush (Dukakis)	52	41	7

Source: Gallup Poll, gathered with the help of James Campbell.

Having observed that results differ even among major polling firms, we might ask whether one firm is more reliable than another. Let us focus on the one poll that called the 1984 presidential race exactly right, Gallup, one of the oldest and most trusted polling organizations. The company began conducting presidential preelection surveys in 1936, when, in contrast to the *Literary Digest,* it forecasted a Roosevelt victory (although it underestimated the Roosevelt vote share by almost 7 percent; see *Gallup Reports*). That forecast helped establish Gallup as a leader in the polling industry. The results from Gallup's final preelection polls for presidential elections since World War II appear in Table 1.3.

How good a forecasting tool is this preelection survey? To help answer the question, imagine you are reading the Gallup results in the newspaper a day or so before the election. That is, you are thinking prospectively, like a true forecaster. Given the reported percentages, and given what you know about sampling error (with a sample of 1,500 we may be 95 percent sure the estimate is right, ± 3 points), for how many elections could you confidently declare a winner? Six: 1952, 1956, 1964, 1972, 1984, and 1988. The other five times the poll results are too close to call, given the potential sampling error. For example, in 1980, the interval would be between 44 and 50 for Reagan and between 41 and 47 for Carter; in other words, before the fact, the Gallup sample could not rule out the possibility that Carter was actually ahead among the voters. (That conclusion is essentially the same, even if we suppose a sampling error of only ± 2, which is about the lower limit statistically.) Also, the conclusion that, prospectively, we are uncertain about the outcomes of five of eleven elections is conservative, since it assumes no other sources of error, such as the real uncertainty over how the "undecideds" will split.

Another shortcoming of the final Gallup presidential preelection poll, when used as a prospective forecasting device, is that its "day before" results provide little lead time. That is, the survey is conducted so close to the contest that it is not a very useful forecast. As Nelson Polsby and Aaron Wildavsky (1984, 206) have put it, "The importance of this kind of prediction is not great. After all, we get to know who has won very soon." There is an inverse relationship between lead time and accuracy. In general, the shorter the lead time, the more accurate the poll. Pollsters, then, are in something of a Catch-22. If they poll early, they enjoy substantial lead time but they risk erroneous forecasts; if they poll late, they reduce error but their lead time is trivial, making the prediction uninteresting. In this sense, the most trivial of all is "exit polling," which takes place on election day itself. (The exit poll has important uses, however, not only to the media networks which depend on it for their election coverage, but also to political scientists interested in studying actual voters; see Frankovic 1990, 2.)

Clearly, scientific polling is not a forecasting panacea.[4] Surveys are simply vulnerable to too many problems. First, the techniques of proper inference require that sampling error margins be assigned to any poll forecasts. Then there are the usual problems of interviewer quality, questionnaire design, and survey execution. Perhaps more seriously, the difficulties of shifting voter intentions constantly intrude. How does one identify who will vote? How does one track the preferences of the voter, which may vary until the last day? The related issue of lead time looms. To be accurate, does the poll have to be so close to the event that it ceases to hold interest? A final drawback is cost. In today's market, companies such as Gallup charge around twenty dollars an interview to conduct and analyze a survey. At this rate, a nationwide presidential poll of 1,500 respondents would cost about $30,000, and the total cost of conducting a separate poll in each of the 435 congressional districts would be an astronomical $13,050,000.

Conclusion

The traditional approaches to forecasting are defective in various ways. The nonscientific forecasters—the prognosticators, the politicos, and the pundits—depend mostly on some combination of luck, intuition, and experience. The pollsters, in contrast, draw heavily on well-developed principles and methods of modern survey research. What separates these sophisticated survey practitioners from academic political scientists is that they are really not concerned with the explanation of elections. Why do voters choose the way they do? What theory can account for an electoral outcome? These are questions that drive students of politics, and they undergird the modeling work that follows. Our forecasting models, which unfold in the next several chapters, are based on what political scientists know (or at least think we know) about electoral behavior. It is hardly surprising, then, that these models would generally do better at forecasting than traditional approaches. We begin with the problem of forecasting presidential election outcomes.

Notes

1. Occasionally a renegade scientist has argued that such "coincidences" are in fact governed by higher-order laws. Austrian biologist Paul Krammerer put forward the "law of seriality," which held that "a coincidence or a series of coincidences is in reality the manifestation of a universal principle in nature which operates independently from the known laws of physical causation" (Koestler 1971, 137). The famous psychologist Carl Jung (1955) shared this view, developing the concept of "synchonicity" as an "acausal connecting principle" underlying coincidences. These cosmic possibilities certainly stimulate the imagination. However, among other difficulties, they cannot account for the inevitable breakdowns of the rules.
2. The bellwether concept derives from the practice of using a bellwether sheep, whereby a bell is put around the neck of the lead male in a flock. The bell signals to the shepherd the direction of the flock.
3. The effect of large numbers is neatly illustrated in the famous statistical puzzle called the birthday problem. How many people need to be in a room in order for the odds to be 50-50 that at least two of them have the same birthday? According to the laws of probability, it is twenty-three ($N = 1.2 \times \sqrt{365 \text{ days}} = 22.9$ days). For three people to have the same birthday, at the same odds, you would need more than 80. Of course, with an extreme number of people, many will have identical birthdays. Statisticians refer to this as the law of truly large numbers; that is, if you have enough cases, just about anything can happen (see Diaconis and Mosteller 1989).
4. Another group of scholars, also disillusioned with the accuracy of public opinion polling, has recently come up with a new alternative: the political stock

market (see Forsythe et al. 1989). These political scientists and economists try to predict the presidential winner on the basis of experiments in which subjects (students) buy or sell stocks representing the candidates. Their Iowa Political Stock Market, on the day before the 1988 election, forecasted Bush's margin of victory with an error of less than 1 percentage point. This accuracy is certainly encouraging, and it was replicated in the 1990 Iowa Senate (Harkin-Tauke) race (Blake 1991). However, there are doubts to be resolved. Aside from the nagging question of whether these student experiments will always generalize to the real world of nationwide electoral choice, there remains the critical issue of lead time. As we have noted, any forecast that appears on the eve of a contest risks being considered trivial.

CHAPTER 2

Presidential Elections: Simple Models

In this chapter, a simple model to forecast presidential election outcomes is developed and evaluated. First, we consider how best to measure candidate performance in an election. A common measure, share of popular vote, is rejected in favor of the tally that ultimately matters, the Electoral College vote share. Success or failure in that body, then, becomes the object of prediction, or forecasting. Drawing on leading findings in the research literature of individual vote choice, we offer preliminary "issues" explanations of presidential results in the post-World War II period. These explanations are constructed and estimated sequentially, looking at possible causes one at a time. This allows salient issues that motivate voters to be carefully examined, along with the accompanying statistical methodology. As will be seen, although the simple relationships uncovered hold promise for forecasting, they finally serve as guideposts to a rather more elaborate model incorporating multiple causes.

Measuring Presidential Election Outcomes

A measure of presidential election outcomes that is widely used by political science researchers is popular vote share. In 1988, for example, Bush received 48,886,097 votes, Dukakis received 41,809,074 votes, and other candidates received 871,768 votes. Measured in percentages, Bush won 53.4 percent, Dukakis 45.7 percent, and alternative party candidates 0.9 percent. If the candidate who received more than 50 percent of the votes always won, it would be easy to distinguish winners from losers. But

Table 2.1 Winning Candidate's Share of the Popular and Electoral Vote, 1948-1988

Year	Winning candidate (party)	(1) Popular vote	(2) Electoral vote
1948	Truman (D)	49.6%	57.1%
1952	Eisenhower (R)	55.1	83.2
1956	Eisenhower (R)	57.4	86.1
1960	Kennedy (D)	49.7	56.4
1964	Johnson (D)	61.1	90.3
1968	Nixon (R)	43.4	55.9
1972	Nixon (R)	60.7	96.7
1976	Carter (D)	50.1	55.2
1980	Reagan (R)	50.7	90.9
1984	Reagan (R)	58.8	97.6
1988	Bush (R)	53.4	79.2

Source: See Appendix.
Note: R = Republican, D = Democratic.

that simple majority rule does not always work. Table 2.1 (column 1) reports the percentage of the popular vote that the winning presidential candidate received for the period 1948-1988. In three of the eleven elections—1948, 1960, and 1968—the victorious candidate failed to garner above 50 percent. Of course, the reason for this failure is that total electoral vote, not total popular vote, determines the victor.

Technically, when Americans vote in presidential elections they are not voting for candidates, they are voting for electors. Each candidate assembles a slate of electors in every state. Electors are usually loyal supporters of the candidate on whose slate they serve. The number of electors per state equals the number of U.S. senators and representatives in the state. For instance, Arizona has two senators and five representatives, for a total of seven electors. The candidate who wins the plurality of popular votes in a state has his or her slate of electors "elected." Thus, in 1988, Bush's slate of electors was elected in Arizona because he won the most popular votes in the state. The candidate who receives the majority of electoral votes nationwide wins. (If no candidate wins enough states to forge a majority, the House of Representatives selects the president, something that has not happened since 1825.) Given the mechanics of the Electoral College, the more accurate definition of presidential election success is the candidate who secures more than 50 percent of the electoral vote.

Since we try to forecast electoral votes directly, rather than concentrating on the more widely used popular vote measure, it is helpful to understand the link between the two approaches. To begin, notice that the

Table 2.2 Incumbent Party's Share of the Popular and Electoral Vote, 1948-1988

Year	Incumbent president (party)	(1) Popular vote	(2) Electoral vote
1948	Truman (D)	49.6%	57.1%
1952	Truman (D)	44.4	16.8
1956	Eisenhower (R)	57.4	86.1
1960	Eisenhower (R)	49.5	40.8
1964	Johnson (D)	61.1	90.3
1968	Johnson (D)	42.7	35.5
1972	Nixon (R)	60.7	96.7
1976	Ford (R)	48.0	44.6
1980	Carter (D)	41.0	9.1
1984	Reagan (R)	58.8	97.6
1988	Reagan (R)	53.4	79.2

Source: See Appendix.

Note: R = Republican, D = Democratic.

percentage of electoral votes amassed by the winners (Table 2.1, column 2) fluctuates far more widely than their percentage of popular vote (column 1). This is a result of the winner-take-all feature of the Electoral College. That is, a candidate picks up all the electoral votes in a state regardless of how large his or her popular vote victory was. For example, Bush won 100.0 percent of the Arizona electoral votes in 1988 even though he polled only 60.8 percent of the popular vote. (Maine is somewhat of an exception in that, in principle, electors may split their vote.)

The winner-take-all aspect of the Electoral College raises the important question of how strong the tie actually is between the popular vote share and the electoral vote share for the nation as a whole. Table 2.2 lists the popular vote share and the Electoral College vote share received by the incumbent party's candidate. (In five of the eleven elections from 1948 to 1988 the incumbent party lost its bid to hold on to the White House.)

When these percentages are plotted on a graph, the relationship between the two variables becomes quite clear. In Figure 2.1, each point represents a candidate and indicates what percentage of the popular vote and electoral vote he received. For example, take the point in the lower left-hand corner. The broken line going down from the point intersects the horizontal axis at about 41 percent of the popular vote, and the broken line running left from the point crosses the vertical axis at about 9 percent of the electoral vote. A quick check of Table 2.2 shows the point stands for Carter's totals in 1980.

Looking at Figure 2.1, we can see that as the incumbent popular vote share gets larger, the electoral vote share tends to get larger. In fact, the

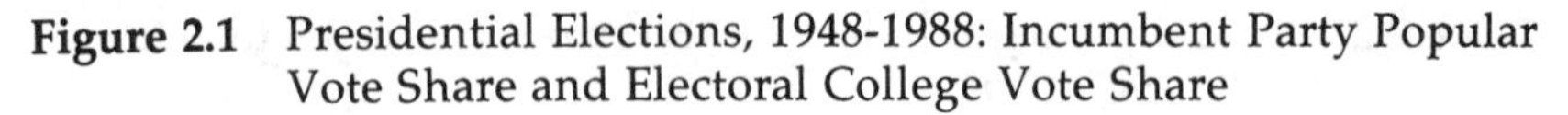

Figure 2.1 Presidential Elections, 1948-1988: Incumbent Party Popular Vote Share and Electoral College Vote Share

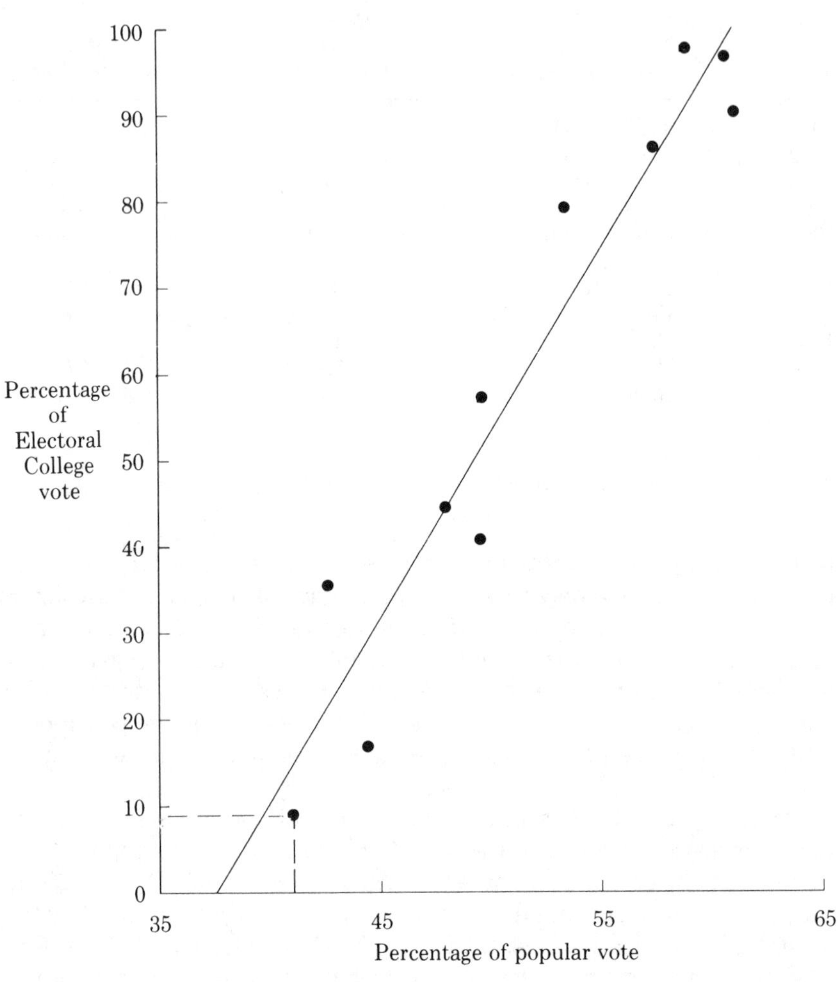

relationship appears rather dependable, with each point near the ascending solid line. This strong relationship can be summarized in a widely used statistical measure called the correlation coefficient or Pearson's r. If the correlation coefficient measures 1.0, the relationship being measured is "perfect," in the sense that all the points fall on the fitted line. If the points are scattered randomly, the expected r value is .00. The correlation coefficient for our relationship in Figure 2.1 is high, r = .96.

Establishing a strong, if imperfect, connection between the Electoral College vote share and the national popular vote share is crucial for our endeavor. In seeking independent variables (or "causes") to account for fluctuations in the electoral vote, we can, with proper caution, draw ideas from the research work that looks more directly at voter choice. Our task, then, is to develop an explanatory model that can forecast electoral vote share.

What Moves Presidential Voters?

Why does a particular voter choose one presidential candidate over another? Political scientists have been, and continue to be, actively engaged in answering this question. Hundreds, not to say thousands, of studies have been published. Most of the work is based on academic election surveys, which were first seriously presented in the classic *The American Voter,* by Angus Campbell, Philip Converse, Warren Miller, and Donald Stokes (1960). From all these efforts, we now have a firmer idea why a voter selects one candidate over the others. One picture that emerges shows that three leading forces shape vote choice in American presidential elections: issues, party identification, and candidate attributes (see Fiorina [1981] and Asher [1988] for good discussions of the vote choice research).

In terms of issues, people tend to vote for candidates who share their views on "important" national and international questions. The meaning of *important* varies from voter to voter, but most voters do have at least a few issues they feel strongly about. For other voters, party identification is the key to vote choice. These individuals pay little attention to the issues or the personal qualities of the candidates, choosing instead to base their votes on party labels. Finally, some studies report that people often decide on whom to vote for after considering the candidates' personal attributes. For instance, candidates who exemplify characteristics such as "honesty" and "integrity" tend to win more support.

The work of electoral behavior scholars forms the foundation of our predictive models. We need to make clear, however, that there are important differences between the vote choice research and our forecasting models. First, the election survey work focuses on accounting for votes that have taken place; for example, one question might be: "How did you vote in the last election?" Sometimes the focus is on votes that will have taken place by the time the research is finished. That is, even if the survey asks, "Who will you vote for in the next election?" the months it takes to administer and tabulate the results almost always eliminate the lead time necessary to generate meaningful explanations in advance of an election contest. Thus, as a practical matter, election surveys serve better for explaining past behavior than for predicting future behavior, which is our purpose.

Second, most of the survey research on voting addresses how an individual decides whom to vote for, rather than how the nation "decides" whom to elect. That is, these election studies are concerned with voting at the individual (micro-) level, not the national (macro-) level. This difference is fundamental. As an analogy, consider the study of unemployment. An economist may be interested in why individuals quit looking for a job (a micro-question) or in why the nation's unemployment rate is rising (a macro-question). Both are legitimate research questions, but they are posed at different levels of analysis. Similarly, in our study, we are finally concerned with the electoral vote share the nation gives a winning presidential candidate, not with how individuals vote.[1]

Given our macro-level forecasting focus, we cannot adopt wholesale the lessons from these micro-level survey studies. Instead, we will have to modify them to fit our collective needs. Take the notion of issue voting, for example. We will need to find a way to translate individuals' issue concerns into national issue measures. Fortunately, this is not as difficult as it may sound. We begin the process by examining issues that move the American voter. The other broad forces that shape choice—party identification and candidate attributes—are joined to issue concerns discussed more fully in Chapter 3.

Issues in the 1984 and 1988 Presidential Elections

In some presidential campaigns, the candidates differ sharply over many issues. The 1964 contest between Barry Goldwater and Lyndon Johnson is an outstanding case. The popular perception of Goldwater was that he wanted to scale back Social Security, block civil rights gains with a strong state's rights stance, confront communism around the globe, strengthen the military, and check federal government growth. Johnson, in contrast, was seen as supporting the expansion of social services and civil rights and as advocating a flexible foreign policy. The conservative Goldwater summed up his issue differences with the liberal Johnson by saying—in what was to become his campaign slogan—that he offered "a choice, not an echo." The electorate responded by giving Johnson a landslide victory over Goldwater. The rejection of the Goldwater "choice" has been widely interpreted as highly ideological and issue-based.

Not all presidential campaigns are as issue-charged as the 1964 contest. The 1976 campaign between Jimmy Carter and Gerald Ford, for instance, is sometimes referred to as the race between tweedle-dum and tweedle-dee, in which policies were rarely discussed. Even such ostensibly bland contests are not without their issues, however. After a careful analysis of the race, Asher (1988, 174) concluded that "there were important issues in 1976, and these tended to work in favor of the

Table 2.3 Issues in the 1984 and 1988 Presidential Campaigns

	Presidential campaign	
Issue type	1984	1988
Social	Abortion School prayer Social Security Tuition tax credit	Abortion School prayer Social Security Pledge of Allegiance Tax breaks for rich Environment Education Health care Drug abuse Gun control Death penalty ACLU/liberalism
Economic	Interest rates Budget deficit Tax increases Economic growth	Number of jobs Budget deficit Tax increases Economic growth
Foreign policy	Lebanon bombing Grenada invasion Central America Soviet relations	Noriega/Panama Iran-contra affair
Personal	Ferraro's finances Reagan's age	Quayle's military record Dukakis's prisoner furlough

Sources: These issue labels were derived from a content analysis of *Newsweek* (September 3, 10, 17, 1984; October 15, 22, 1984; September 5, 12, 19, 26, 1988; October 3, 10, 17, 24, 31, 1988).

Democrats." In particular, Ford and the Republicans were blamed for the sluggish economy.

Issues were also at the forefront of the two most recent presidential campaigns. Reagan and Mondale sparred openly in 1984 over how to lower the deficit and how to deal with the Soviets. Four years later, Bush and Dukakis had very different ideas about what role the federal government should play in promoting education, health care, and environmental protection. And the deficit still loomed as a major concern.

A systematic list of the major issues in the 1984 and 1988 campaigns is presented in Table 2.3. They are grouped into four broad categories: social, economic, foreign policy, and personal. The particular issues were culled from a content analysis of *Newsweek* magazine. We can see that the weekly news source reported on a wide variety of concerns in both campaigns. Beyond this, it is important to notice that some of the issues surfaced in both races, while others were unique to one election. Among the social issues, a few, like abortion, made the news in both 1984 and 1988. But many others, like tuition tax credits and gun control, were reported on during only one campaign. The foreign policy and personal issues were even more idiosyncratic. Among the broad issue categories, only under economics do we find much consistency; the deficit, tax increases, and economic growth were important concerns in both years.

The stability of economic issues across the two campaigns suggests they may be especially useful in forecasting. That is, if voters respond to the economy in every campaign, then perhaps an economic indicator could be related systematically to election outcomes over time. Before checking for a link, however, we need to confirm that the economy is on voters' minds year after year. We also need to determine which economic issues consistently trouble voters. Fortunately, Gallup has data that will help us with both these tasks.

Every year since 1948, the Gallup organization has asked Americans, What "is the most important problem facing this country today?" The top three responses by year are displayed in Table 2.4. It shows that economic issues—unemployment, inflation, government spending, general economic problems, and the deficit—have been pervasive. Marked in bold, they show up almost every year. Quite often, two of the three most important problems have been economic in nature. Moreover, the same ones often appear. For example, the high cost of living (inflation) made the list in twenty-one of the forty-two years, and unemployment broke into the top three eighteen times.

No other class of issues exhibits such staying power across this 1948-1989 period. Foreign policy matters appeared almost as often as economic issues, but the particular foreign policy concerns changed dramatically with the times. The general fear of war was a concern primarily in the 1950s and early 1980s. The Korean War was the top issue in 1952 and 1953, and the Vietnam War dominated the rankings in the late 1960s and early 1970s. Global foreign problems were important periodically, and a few specific international issues surfaced just once, such as Sputnik in 1958 and Cuba in 1963. Social issues were listed as serious problems only occasionally. Civil rights (integration and race relations) was cited nine times from the mid-1950s to the late 1960s. Crime appeared five times, and dissatisfaction with government (corruption in government) showed up four times. Most other social issues were mentioned no more than once or twice.

The Gallup data establish that economic issues, more consistently than any other issue set, have been on the minds of American voters throughout the past four decades. Armed with this evidence, we take up an examination of the relationship between the economy and elections. (For current research literature on this relationship, see Norpoth, Lewis-

Table 2.4 "Most Important Problem" Over Time, 1948-1989

Year	Most important problem	Second most important problem	Third most important problem
1948	**Inflation**	Marshall Plan	Soviets
1949	Preventing war	**Unemployment**	**Cost of living**
1950	Preventing war	**Inflation**	**Unemployment**
1951	War	**Economic problems**	Govt. corruption
1952	Korean War	Govt. corruption	**Inflation**
1953	Korean War	**High taxes**	Avoiding World War III
1954	Foreign relations	**Economic problems**	**Unemployment**
1955	Foreign policy	Communism in US	**Economic problems**
1956	Threat of war	Civil rights	**Cost of living**
1957	Keeping out of war	**Cost of living**	Integration
1958	Keeping peace	**Economic problems**	Sputnik
1959	Keeping peace	**Unemployment**	Integration
1960	Missile gap	Foreign problems	**Economic problems**
1961	Soviets	**Cost of living**	**Economic problems**
1962	War	**Cost of living**	**Unemployment**
1963	Cuba	Foreign problems	**Unemployment**
1964	Racial problems	Foreign problems	**Unemployment**
1965	Vietnam	Civil rights	Threat of war
1966	Vietnam	**Cost of living**	Civil rights
1967	Vietnam	Civil rights	**Cost of living**
1968	Vietnam	Race relations	Crime
1969	Vietnam	Crime	Race relations
1970	Campus unrest	Vietnam	Foreign problems
1971	Vietnam	**Economic problems**	Foreign problems
1972	Vietnam	**Inflation**	Drugs
1973	**Cost of living**	Drugs	Crime
1974	Energy crisis	**Cost of living**	Govt. corruption
1975	**Cost of living**	**Unemployment**	Govt. corruption
1976	**Cost of living**	**Unemployment**	Crime
1977	**Cost of living**	**Unemployment**	Energy problems
1978	**Cost of living**	Energy problems	**Unemployment**
1979	**Cost of living**	Foreign problems	Energy problems
1980	Foreign problems	**Cost of living**	Energy problems
1981	**Cost of living**	**Unemployment**	Crime
1982	**Cost of living**	**Unemployment**	Budget cuts
1983	**Unemployment**	**Inflation**	Fear of war
1984	Threat of war	**Unemployment**	Govt. spending
1985	Threat of war	**Unemployment**	Govt. spending
1986	Foreign tensions	**Unemployment**	**Federal deficit**
1987	**Unemployment**	**Federal deficit**	**Economic problems**
1988	**Federal deficit**	**Economic problems**	Drugs
1989	**Economic problems**	Drugs	**Poverty**

Source: Gallup Poll (various issues).

Note: Economic problems are boldfaced.

Beck, and Lafay 1991.) After evaluating that connection, we return to consideration of noneconomic issues as well.

The Impact of Economic Issues

To further our understanding of the link between the macroeconomy and national election outcomes, we inspect the psychological bond of economic concerns and individual vote choice. Scholars have employed election survey data to demonstrate that a person's evaluation of the economy does influence who he or she favors for president (see, among others, Fiorina 1981; Kiewiet 1983). To illustrate, consider the work by one of us, Michael Lewis-Beck (1988b, 124-126) on the 1984 presidential campaign. An explanatory model of vote choice for that contest was proposed as follows, in words,

$$\begin{matrix}\text{Vote} \\ \text{choice}\end{matrix} = \begin{matrix}\text{National} \\ \text{economic} \\ \text{evaluation}\end{matrix} + \begin{matrix}\text{Party} \\ \text{identification}\end{matrix} \qquad \text{(Eq. 2.1)}$$

This model says that an individual's decision on whom to vote for was determined by his or her perception of national economic conditions and party identification. (Candidate attributes was omitted because of the lack of a satisfactory measure. In the statistical estimation, social status variables were included to help take account of, or control for, these and other possible variables.)

The particular issue of interest here is economic performance. The rationale behind the economic evaluations measure employed in this model is straightforward. Before an election, people supposedly assess the state of the national economy. If they conclude that times are good, they vote for the incumbent president (or the candidate of the president's party). If they think times are bad, they vote against the incumbent president (or the candidate of the president's party). A number of survey questions have been designed to uncover this reasoning. The query used by Lewis-Beck (1988b, 125), from the Survey of Consumer Attitudes (at the University of Michigan), is as follows: "As to the economic policy of the government—I mean steps taken to fight inflation and unemployment—would you say the government is doing a good job, only fair, or a poor job?" When respondents selected through a nationwide probability sample were asked this question before the 1984 presidential election, the results showed an unmistakable link between vote intention and the perception of economic policy. Respondents who said the government was doing a "good job" fighting inflation and unemployment were 44 percent more likely to vote for President Reagan than were those who

Table 2.5 Evaluation of the National Economy and Presidential Vote Choice, 1988 National Election Survey

	Evaluation of the national economy		
Vote intention	"Worse"	"Same"	"Better"
Bush	36%	54%	75%
Dukakis	64	46	25
	100%	100%	100%
Number of respondents	(517)	(836)	(329)

Source: The 1988 National Election Survey, University of Michigan.

Note: The vote question was: "Who do you think you will vote for in the elections for President?" The economic evaluation question was: "How about the economy. Would you say that over the past year the nation's economy has gotten better, stayed about the same, or gotten worse?" Read the table left to right, across the economic categories, to see how vote preference for Bush increases as the economic evaluation improves.

said the government was doing a "poor job" (regardless of their party attachment or social status; see Lewis-Beck 1988b, 133-135). The analysis suggests strongly that voters' positive evaluations of the economy contributed heavily to the Reagan landslide. Other scholars, using different data sets, have reached the same conclusion (Frankovic 1985; Kiewiet and Rivers 1985; Lipset 1985).

For the 1988 presidential election, the story can be told in much the same way. Table 2.5 displays the relationship between economic evaluations and vote intention, according to the 1988 National Election Survey. This time the following economic question was posed to respondents: "Would you say that over the past year the nation's economy has gotten better, stayed the same, or gotten worse?"

The data show that, in general, the more favorably a person viewed the performance of the economy over the preelection year, the more likely he or she was to vote for the incumbent party candidate, George Bush. Specifically, Bush won the support of only 36 percent of the respondents who thought the economy had gotten worse, in contrast to 75 percent of those who thought the economy had improved. One interesting implication is that Dukakis might have won the election if more people had rated the economy as doing worse!

Since a strong relationship between vote choice and economic evaluation exists at the individual level, we should not be surprised to find one at the national level. We have already fixed our macro-level elections measure, that is, the incumbent party electoral vote share. What about a macroeconomic measure? The Gallup "most important problem"

Table 2.6 Unemployment Rate Change and Presidential Election Outcomes, 1948-1988

Incumbent party candidate is:	Unemployment rate: March to June[a] Falling	Steady or rising
Winner	Truman, 1948 Johnson, 1964 Nixon, 1972 Reagan, 1984 Bush, 1988	Eisenhower, 1956
Loser	Nixon, 1960	Stevenson, 1952 Humphrey, 1968 Ford, 1976 Carter, 1980

Source: Department of Labor, various bulletins.

[a]Indicates the change in the unemployment rate from March to June of the election year. The calculation is a percentage change from period to period. For example, if unemployment increased from 4 to 5 percent, the change score would be 25 percent. The change scores for the years in the table are: 1948 = −10.0; 1952 = 3.6; 1956 = 2.4; 1960 = −1.9; 1964 = −3.8; 1968 = 0.0; 1972 = −3.5; 1976 = 0.0; 1980 = 21.0; 1984 = −6.6; 1988 = −5.5. A positive score indicates that the unemployment rate worsened over the March to June period.

poll data suggest two possibilities, for unemployment and inflation received the most mentions. Unemployment seems especially relevant, since in 1946 Congress passed the Full Employment Act, giving government officials responsibility for holding down joblessness. As an experiment, suppose we test the following simple hypothesis:

> When the unemployment rate is falling (rising), the incumbent party will win (lose).

The results of the 1948-1988 data in Table 2.6 show that when the unemployment rate fell prior to the election, the incumbent party won five elections and lost one. In contrast, when the unemployment rate did not improve, the incumbent party lost four contests and won just one.

Thus, the unemployment hypothesis holds up well. However, this unemployment measure is one macroeconomic indicator among many. Furthermore, the overall tightness of its relationship to electoral vote share, as measured by a Pearson's r = −.64, is equaled or exceeded by several other relevant indicators. Table 2.7 reports the correlation coefficients between the electoral vote and a series of common macroeconomic variables: unemployment, inflation, income, and gross national product (GNP), each measured for different time periods. Clearly,

Table 2.7 Correlation (Pearson's r) Between Macroeconomic Measures and the Electoral Vote

Economic variable	Correlation with electoral vote
Change in unemployment	
March to June	−.64
December to June	−.57
June to June	−.57
Change in inflation	
March to June	−.41
December to June	−.39
June to June	−.50
Change in personal income	
1st quarter to 2d quarter	.37
4th quarter to 2d quarter	.46
2d quarter to 2d quarter	.66
Change in GNP	
1st quarter to 2d quarter	.66
4th quarter to 2d quarter	.69
2d quarter to 2d quarter	.62

Source: See Appendix.

Note: Monthly changes are from March to June of the election year, December the year before the election to June of the election year, and June of the year before the election to June of the election year. Quarterly changes are from first quarter (January-March) to second quarter (April-June) of the election year, fourth quarter (October-December) of the year before the election to second quarter of the election year, and second quarter of the year before the election to second quarter of the election year.

regardless of the one selected, macroeconomic performance appears firmly joined to electoral vote share. Also noteworthy is the fact that none of the correlations is close to 1.0. This suggests, not surprisingly, that other issues in addition to economics mold presidential election outcomes.

The Impact of Noneconomic Issues

An old presidential campaign adage contends that to win, a candidate must convince voters that he or she will deliver peace and prosperity. We have just confirmed that economic prosperity is related to electoral success for the incumbent. How about peace? For example, the unpopular Vietnam War contributed to Johnson's decision not to seek reelection in 1968. Likewise, the frustrating Iran hostage crisis eventually turned voters away from Carter in 1980. Overall, defense and foreign policy issues do seem to count, for they make Gallup's "most important problem" list in thirty of the forty-two years (refer back to Table 2.4).

A wide array of social issues can also influence vote choice. Kennedy's Catholicism helped shape voters' decisions in 1960 (Converse et al. 1966), and civil rights played a major role in determining their decisions in 1964 (Campbell 1966) and 1968 (Converse et al. 1969). More recently, Bush exploited the issues of law and order to his advantage in 1988 (Pomper 1989). Finally, personal concerns—such as Reagan's age in 1984 and Quayle's military record in 1988—can sway a few voters.

As election forecasters, the question we face is how to find usable macro-level measures of these various issues: economic, social, foreign, and personal. The first is not so difficult, for long-established economic indicators are readily available. But for the other issue areas, no such indicators are available. For instance, there is no "national social problems index" for society, comparable to, say, the gross national product for measuring the economy.

Nevertheless, there is one measure which, we believe, can be considered something of a global indicator of how the president is handling the issues, economic or not. That is the monthly Gallup Poll presidential approval question. The question reads: "Do you approve or disapprove of the way ______ is handling his job as president?"

The results of this query, commonly but perhaps misleadingly referred to as presidential popularity, have been used by numerous scholars (see, for example, Kernell 1977; Mackuen 1983; Mueller 1973; Norpoth 1985; Ostrom and Simon 1985). Our notion is that voters who agree with the president on the issues will register that agreement by approving of the way he is handling his job.

Obviously, presidential approval would be partially determined by the economic issues we have already studied. However, we also suppose a fair portion of presidential approval to be driven by social, foreign, and personal issues. If so, then we would expect two things. First, macroeconomic performance is clearly, but not powerfully, correlated with presidential approval. In fact, this is the case. When the most potent macroeconomic variable of Table 2.7, GNP growth (fourth to second quarter), is correlated with presidential approval, $r = .48$. This suggests that, while popularity is influenced by the economy, it is by no means dominated by it. Certainly, other, noneconomic issues play a role in shaping presidential approval.

The second expectation is that presidential approval, because it is a broader issue measure, would correlate more highly with electoral vote share than the macroeconomic variables. This would be especially encouraging in light of our forecasting goals. To examine the tie between presidential popularity and elections, we compared summer approval ratings to actual election outcomes for the post-World War II period. The

Table 2.8 Presidential Popularity and Presidential Election Outcomes, 1948-1988

	Presidential popularity: July approval	Average presidential popularity: Winners vs. losers
Incumbent party winners		
1948 Truman	39%	
1956 Eisenhower	69	
1964 Johnson	74	Incumbent winners' average = 57%
1972 Nixon	56	
1984 Reagan	52	
1988 Bush	51	
Incumbent party losers		
1952 Stevenson	32	
1960 Nixon	49	Incumbent losers' average = 37%
1968 Humphrey	40	
1976 Ford	45	
1980 Carter	21	

Source: See Appendix.

Note: Presidential approval ratings are from the July Gallup Poll conducted in the summer before the election. The average scores are the mean popularity measures within the winning and losing groups.

results are presented in Table 2.8. Looking first at popularity, we see that it ranged widely. Johnson, for example, enjoyed a July 1964 rating of 74 percent, while Carter scored only 21 percent in July 1980. Johnson followed up his high approval rating with a big win, and Carter's low mark was precursor to a big defeat. As suggestive as these extremes are, we need to consider all elections. An overview is presented in the final column of Table 2.8. On average, when the incumbent party won reelection the sitting president had a summer approval score of 57 percent, but when the incumbent lost that rating stood at just 37 percent.

Figure 2.2 displays the relationship between popularity and election outcomes visually. Scores on the variable of presidential approval are marked along the horizontal axis, that of the incumbent party electoral vote share along the vertical axis. The points, each of which represents the approval-vote results for a particular election, align in a tidy upward-sloping pattern. The correlation between the two variables is large, $r = .84$, larger than that of the macroeconomic variables. Clearly, the more the public approves of the president prior to the election, the more likely the incumbent party is to retain control of the White House.

So far we have studied only the tie between July ratings and election outcomes. Figure 2.3 goes a step further, reporting the correlations

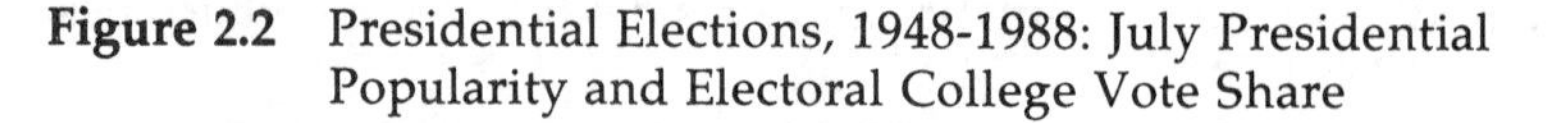

Figure 2.2 Presidential Elections, 1948-1988: July Presidential Popularity and Electoral College Vote Share

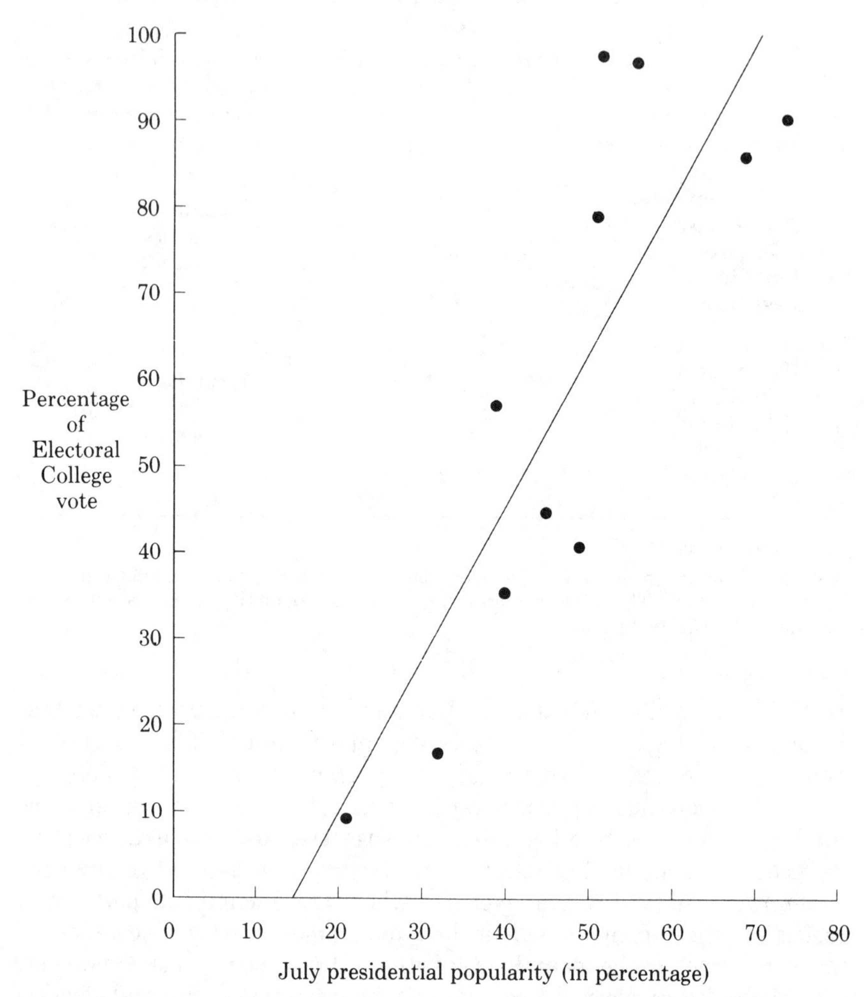

between the Gallup presidential approval scores and the electoral vote share at different times. The r values indicate that popularity is linked closely to outcomes as early as eighteen months before the balloting. As election day approaches the strength of the relationship increases, culminating in the summer months. Indeed, it peaks with the July popularity measure.

Curiously, the r values in Figure 2.3 weaken slightly after the July high point. Is this just a fluke of the data? Probably not. When the popularity measures are correlated with the popular vote share (rather

Figure 2.3 Correlation Between Presidential Approval and Incumbent Electoral Vote Share, 1948-1988

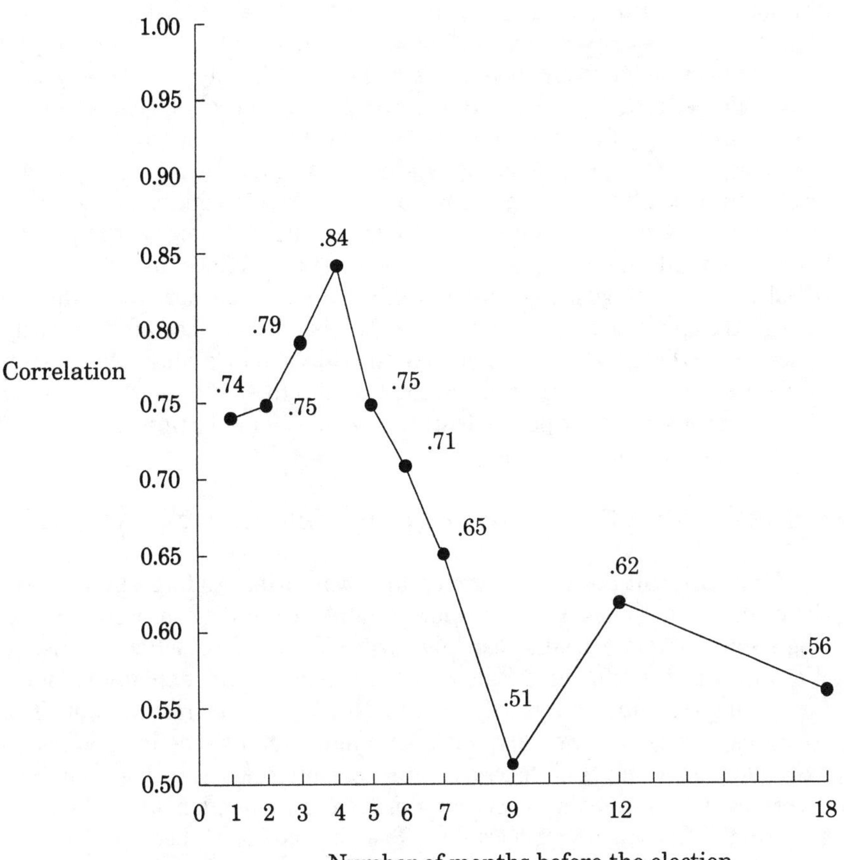

Source: See Appendix.

Note: Percent approval in the presidential Gallup Poll is correlated (Pearson's r) with the actual electoral vote share for the incumbent party candidate. The months in question are: 18 = May (of year before election); 12 = November (of year before election); 9 = February; 7 = April; 6 = May; 5 = June; 4 = July; 3 = August; 2 = September; 1 = October.

than electoral vote share), the same pattern emerges. (Interestingly, a similar pattern surfaces in French elections, which we explore in Chapter 8.) Assuming this connection is real, it is certainly advantageous to forecasters, permitting a healthy lead time in making predictions for an upcoming race.

Still, why does the relationship exist? After all, it seems counterintuitive. Shouldn't popularity measured just before the vote, say in October, better reflect preferences than a measure taken in midsummer? Maybe not. From Labor Day until the November balloting, the campaign heats up. Many conflicting, superficial, sudden signals are sent out to the voter, almost like flares in the night. These extremely short-term forces pull certain voters away from their preferred choice, if only momentarily. Of these many effects, those from the televised presidential debates seem the classic example, generating quick booms and busts in candidate support. One result is that a core group shifts its presidential rating, however briefly. Statistically speaking, such shifts create unreliability in the presidential popularity measures close to the contest. That is, the figures bounce around more. (Specifically, the average change in presidential popularity from August to October is 4.2 points; in contrast, from June to August the average change is only 1.6 points). Thus, the fall popularity figures immediately before the election tend to produce somewhat greater prediction error, as suggested in Figure 2.3. In the end, the summer measure provides a sharper assessment of presidential approval.

Presidential Popularity: A Simple Forecasting Exercise

The apparent power of summer approval ratings to foretell presidential election outcomes warrants more rigorous examination. Perhaps this single explanatory variable can give us sufficient forecasting precision. We will explore this possibility, at the same time explaining some forecasting techniques that will serve us throughout the rest of book. The statistical procedure we rely on to estimate our forecasting models is regression analysis. Simple regression analysis finds the line that best describes the relationship between a predicted (dependent) variable, and a predictor (independent) variable. The line is "best" because it minimizes the error. (In Figure 2.2, imagine the total error as the sum of the distances from the points to the line, squared so their signs will not cancel each other out.) Expressed as an equation, the line can be used to generate election forecasts.[2]

The regression line of Figure 2.2 is represented in the following equation:

$$V = -25.52 + 1.77PP \qquad \text{(Eq. 2.2)}$$

where V = electoral vote; PP = presidential popularity measured in the July Gallup Poll before the election.

The number 1.77 estimates the slope of the line and quantifies the predictive connection between the two variables, percentage presidential approval and percentage electoral vote. It suggests how much the electoral vote changes in response to popularity change. In particular, it says that for every additional 1.00 percentage point jump in presidential approval, the incumbent party candidate can expect to pick up 1.77 percentage points more of the electoral vote. The other number in the equation, −25.52, is a constant. (Imagine where the line in Figure 2.2 would intercept the vertical axis, if it continued.) Whenever a prediction of the electoral vote is made on the basis of a given popularity score, this constant must be added in; otherwise, the prediction can be expected to miss by that amount. In other words, one can think of this constant as an added term that makes things come out right.

With this basic understanding of equation 2.2, we can make electoral vote predictions for specific candidates. For example, when presidential popularity is 21 percent, the Carter score for 1980, the predicted electoral vote share is 11.7 percent.

$$\begin{aligned} V &= -25.52 + 1.77(21) \\ &= -25.52 + 37.17 \\ &= 11.7 \end{aligned}$$

The actual electoral vote share Carter received was 9.1 percent. Comparing this actual electoral vote share (V) to the predicted share ($\hat{V}$) yields a prediction error (PE) of −2.6 percentage points.

$$\begin{aligned} PE &= V - \hat{V} \qquad \text{(Eq. 2.3)} \\ &= 9.1 - 11.7 \\ &= -2.6 \end{aligned}$$

Employing equation 2.2, we can predict each of the eleven post-World War II presidential elections and calculate the prediction error for each (with equation 2.3). The results of these computations are presented in Table 2.9. Observe that the prediction errors (column 4) range from −20.4 in 1960 to 31.1 in 1984. Viewed in absolute terms (without positive or negative designation) the errors in Table 2.9 run from only 2.6 in 1980 to 31.1 in 1984.

This range of scores tells us something about the spread of errors, but it fails to provide much sense of the typical amount of error. For that, we calculate the average absolute prediction error (APE) across all the elections. In this case (see Table 2.9) APE = 14.95. Thus, on average, the presidential popularity forecasting model was off about 15 percent.

Another common summary measure of prediction error is the standard error of estimate (SEE). This measure is more appropriate for judging the typical amount of error when the forecaster wishes to predict an election out of sample (in this case, one that does not occur between 1948 and 1988), such as the upcoming presidential contest. For the data in Table 2.9, SEE = 18.4 percent, suggesting even more error than that implied by the APE of 14.95.[3]

Table 2.9 Prediction Accuracy of Electoral Vote Outcomes from Presidential Popularity, 1948-1988

Incumbent Electoral Vote = −25.52 + 1.77 (popularity)

Year	Incumbent party candidate (party)	(1) July approval	(2) Model prediction	(3) Actual electoral share	(4) Prediction error (3) − (2)
1948	Truman (D)	39%	43.5%	57.1%	13.6%
1952	Stevenson (D)	32	31.1	16.8	−14.3
1956	Eisenhower (R)	69	96.6	86.1	−10.5
1960	Nixon (R)	49	61.2	40.8	−20.4
1964	Johnson (D)	74	105.5	90.3	−15.2
1968	Humphrey (D)	40	45.3	35.5	−9.8
1972	Nixon (R)	56	73.6	96.7	23.1
1976	Ford (R)	45	54.1	44.6	−9.5
1980	Carter (D)	21	11.7	9.1	−2.6
1984	Reagan (R)	52	66.5	97.6	31.1
1988	Bush (R)	51	64.8	79.2	14.4

Source: See Appendix.

Notes: The candidate of the incumbent presidential party (R = Republican, D = Democratic) is listed. Column 1 is the percentage approval in the July Gallup poll. Column 2 is the electoral share prediction from the popularity equation (equation 2.2). Column 4 is the prediction error, calculated by subtracting a candidate's predicted electoral vote share (column 2) from the actual share (column 3). The APE (average absolute prediction error) = 14.95. The APE is calculated by adding the absolute values of the scores in column 4 and dividing by 11 (the number of scores).

The APE and SEE help determine the performance of our regression model. When the goal is to forecast, the smaller the APE and SEE, the better the model. Measured against these criteria, how well does our July popularity regression model (equation 2.2) perform? Not that well. The APE (14.95) and SEE (18.4) are simply too large to afford us much confidence in predicting future elections. These measures, then, quantify what is visible in Figure 2.2: the election points stray too far from the regression line. Clearly, presidential popularity, despite its premier status as a surrogate variable for a host of leading issues, cannot by itself generate exceptionally accurate forecasts.

Conclusion

When individual Americans vote in a presidential election, their choices are ultimately expressed as an outcome in the Electoral College. To predict successfully the incumbent's electoral vote share, it is useful to find national-level measures of the variables that motivate individual voters. In this chapter, we identified leading aggregate measures of issues—economic and noneconomic—and related them to the electoral vote. Various macroeconomic indicators—unemployment, inflation, disposable income, and GNP—correlate nicely with incumbent party performance. Presidential popularity, as expressed in the Gallup Poll approval ratings, taps economic and noneconomic concerns well. That measure is even more highly correlated with electoral vote share than are the various economic indicators. Nevertheless, presidential popularity is not potent enough to stand alone in a forecasting equation. More complete, multivariate models, combining issue measures with other central vote determinants, are needed. This is the task to be accomplished in Chapter 3.

Notes

1. An erroneous judgment about the behavior of individuals made on the basis of observations of aggregate behavior (such as whole nations) is called an ecological fallacy. For example, suppose someone observes a correlation between national GNP growth and national incumbent electoral vote share, then claims that individual citizens are voting on the basis of their own economic circumstances. That deduction, from the nation to the individual, may commit the ecological fallacy. Individual voters may not be responding to their personal economic welfare. Rather, they may be responding to something else, such as candidate quality, which is positively correlated with economic growth and more votes (on this argument, see especially Jacobson 1983, chap. 6). Only by looking at individual voters' opinions, such as in an election survey, can the scholar begin to sort out these individual decision-making mechanisms. In fact, the overwhelming evidence is that American voters hardly respond to their pocketbooks; instead, they seem to care mostly about the nation's economic well-being (see Lewis-Beck 1988b, chap. 3).

   Fortunately, here we need not overly concern ourselves with the ecological fallacy problem. Since our goal is prediction of the national election result, it is sufficient to demonstrate that the national economic-electoral link exists. In sum, our research is about the overall election outcome, not the individual voter's decision. As Lutz Erbring (1989, 267) sagely observed: "It is worth remembering that there are significant research questions in the social sciences that are macrotheoretical to begin with ... in terms of politically relevant collective experiences, conditions, events or outcomes."

   In specifying our macro-level models, we have borrowed freely from the research findings on individual voting behavior. Our models of national action correspond, we believe, with models of individual action. However, the consistency of this aggregation, from individual to collectivity, may be impossible to demonstrate empirically and/or theoretically, according to some scholars (but see King 1990a). A parallel problem exists in the field of economics, with the difficulties of establishing micro foundations for macroeconomic models (see Paldam 1991, 26-29). The frequent isomorphism between individuals and nations might best be viewed as a heuristic, or intuitive, way of thinking about how the models work.

2. Regression analysis is probably the most widely used statistical tool in political science research. In this book, we strive to give the reader a good working knowledge of how to interpret regression results. However, full justice to the technical issues cannot be given here. In particular, we have had to sacrifice discussion of the critical assumptions on which the procedure rests. For a deeper understanding of regression a text should be consulted. A beginning volume is Lewis-Beck (1980a). More advanced treatments, in order, are available in Berry and Feldman (1985), Kelejian and Oates (1974), Fox (1991), and Pindyck and Rubinfeld (1990).

   It is easy enough to show how to find a simple regression line, such as that in Figure 2.2. Recall from high school algebra that the general equation for a line can be written

$$Y = a + bX$$

To find the particular best-fitting line relating two variables, X and Y, a and b can be calculated as follows:

$$b = \frac{\Sigma(X_i - \overline{X})(Y_i - \overline{Y})}{\Sigma(X_i - \overline{X})^2}$$

where b = the slope of the line; Σ = sum; X_i = observations on variable X; $\overline{X}$ = mean of X; Y_i = observations on variable Y; $\overline{Y}$ = mean of Y. Then

$$a = \overline{Y} - b\overline{X}$$

where a = the intercept, or constant. These two calculated values for a and b, such as −25.52 and 1.77, respectively, from equation 2.2, allow the fitting of a line that is best in that it minimizes the sum of the squares of the errors, as follows:

$$SSE = \Sigma(Y_i - \hat{Y}_i)^2$$

where SSE = the sum of the squares of the errors; Y_i = observations on variable Y; $\hat{Y}_i$ = predicted values for variable Y.

3. The formula for the standard error of estimate for equation 2.2 is as follows:

$$SEE = \sqrt{\frac{\Sigma(Y_i - \hat{Y})^2}{N - 2}}$$

$$= 18.4$$

where SEE = the standard error of estimate; Y = V (electoral vote share); $\hat{Y} = \hat{V}$ (predicted electoral vote share).

   This figure can be used to construct a forecast interval for specific future predictions. To see how it works, assume that Bush's popularity in July 1992 is 52 percent. Employing equation 2.2, we would predict that the Republican nominee (presumably Bush himself) would garner 66.5 percent of the electoral vote. From statistical theory, the SEE suggests that we can be about 68 percent confident that the actual vote share will be within $\pm$ 18.4 percentage points of 66.5 (that is, between 48.1 and 84.9). Construction of such confidence intervals can give us a sense of how far off a forecast is likely to be. (Given a specific value on a predictor variable, a somewhat more precise but not necessarily narrower interval may be calculated, at the price of considerably more calculation; see Abraham and Ledolter 1983; Kelejian and Oates 1974, 111-116.)

CHAPTER 3

Presidential Elections: More Complete Models

A simple forecasting model based on the lone variable of presidential popularity is informative but insufficient. Instead, we need a model with more than one explanatory variable. Not surprisingly, presidential election success, like most political phenomena, turns out to be multicausal. Here we explore different multivariate explanations. The first relies exclusively on the role of issues, extending themes developed in the previous chapter. After we have tested the limits of an all-issues model, we incorporate the effects of the other major vote determinants, party loyalty and candidate appeal. By chapter's end, we are able to offer a presidential forecasting model of considerable theoretical and statistical power.

An Issues Model of Presidential Elections

Thus far, we have considered how various types of issues—economic, social, foreign, personal—can affect individual vote choice in presidential elections. One parsimonious grouping of these concerns leads to the following basic multivariate issues model:

$$\text{Individual vote} = \text{Economic} + \text{Noneconomic issues} \quad \text{(Eq. 3.1)}$$

Such a model suggests that citizens evaluate performance on economic and noneconomic issues before deciding how to vote. If they are satisfied overall, they vote for the incumbent president or the candidate of the incumbent presidential party. Otherwise, they vote against the incumbent party's candidate.

Table 3.1 Correlations Between Economic Measures

	Change in:		
Change in:	Inflation	Personal income	GNP
Unemployment	.71	−.65	−.82
Inflation		−.44	−.43
Personal Income			.65

Source: See Appendix.

Note: The changes in unemployment and inflation are from December of the year before the election to June of the election year, and the changes in personal income and GNP are from the fourth quarter of the year before the election to the second quarter of the election year.

To translate this basic micro-level model into a macro-level forecasting model, we need to find proxy variables for economic and noneconomic issues. It is easy enough to find a proxy for the first, as an array of appropriate macroeconomic indicators is available. However, the second may seem more problematic. The presidential popularity variable of Chapter 2 certainly taps noneconomic issues but, as noted, it also taps economic ones. Ideally, we would like to take the strictly economic component out of the popularity measure, thus leaving an altered measure of popularity that varied only with noneconomic issues. Fortunately, multiple regression analysis (as opposed to bivariate regression) allows the imposition of statistical controls. This means that the estimation of a properly specified model, including a sound measure of economic performance along with presidential popularity, can separate out the economic component of the latter. Thus, the effect of noneconomic issues, as measured through presidential approval, can be assessed independent of economic conditions. The following description for the macro-level multivariate forecasting model, then, readily suggests itself:

$$\text{Electoral vote share} = \text{Economic conditions} + \text{Presidential popularity} \qquad \text{(Eq. 3.2)}$$

The model asserts that the presidential party's share of the electoral vote is predicted from a combination of these two variables. As a measure of presidential popularity, we employ the Gallup percentage approval measure just explored in equation 2.2. In measuring economic performance, there are many possibilities to choose from. We rely on the more global macroeconomic indicator of growth rate of the gross national product (GNP), which, as can be seen from the correlations in Table 3.1, largely measures the other relevant indicators (unemployment, inflation, or income).

To estimate the model, we apply multiple regression (ordinary least squares) to the 1948-1988 data set, which yields

$$V = -20.90 + 6.83{*}G + 1.40{*}PP \qquad \text{(Eq. 3.3)}$$
$$(-1.26) \quad (2.04) \quad (3.75)$$

$R^2 = .81$ $N = 11$
SEE $= 15.82$ D-W $= 1.63$

where V = incumbent party's percentage share of electoral vote; G = percentage change in real GNP over six months prior (from the fourth quarter in the year before the election to the second quarter of the election year); PP = approval percentage for the president in July of the election year (from Gallup Poll); R^2 = coefficient of multiple determination; N = the number of cases; SEE = the standard error of the estimate; D-W = the Durbin-Watson statistic; the values in parentheses are t-ratios; * = statistically significant at .05, one-tail, $|t| > 1.86$.

The coefficients next to G and PP (6.83 and 1.40, respectively) are slope estimates. In principle, multiple regression gets these estimates in the same way as the simple regression of the last chapter, finding a line that best fits a scatter of points. Of course, the error-minimizing "line" is now a plane, since another dimension has been added to the picture. Further, because two variables offer a better explanation than just one, such as popularity, these slope estimates will be more accurate. (Technically, they will be less biased. The popularity coefficient will be closer to the truth, as compared with equation 2.2, as will the GNP coefficient, which was effectively zero in equation 2.2.) Interpreting such estimates and the accompanying statistics is straightforward. We will go over them step by step, since they provide basic information needed here and elsewhere.

Because of the forecasting goal, it is important to understand how to use equation 3.3 to generate predictions. Simply plug in the appropriate GNP and popularity figures for a given contest, and solve. Take, for instance, the 1948 election between incumbent Democrat Harry Truman and Republican Thomas Dewey. Most political observers of the day called this race for Dewey. What would be the prediction using equation 3.3? A check of the relevant GNP and popularity data (see the Appendix) shows that Truman's approval stood at a only 39 percent in July, but GNP growth was a healthy 2.42 percent. Thus, when we solve by substituting in these numbers for PP and G, respectively, the arithmetic yields:

$$\begin{aligned}\text{1948 vote prediction} &= \text{Constant} + 6.83\,(\text{1948 GNP score}) + 1.40\,(\text{1948 popularity score})\\ &= -20.90 + 6.83(2.42) + 1.40(39)\\ &= -20.90 + 16.53 + 54.60\\ &= 50.23\\ &= \text{win for incumbent Truman}\end{aligned}$$

Not only do the results forecast accurately Truman's narrow victory, they also suggest why he won. The GNP boom implies that voters would approve of his performance on economic issues. At the same time, his poor popularity rating indicates that the voters were dissatisfied with him on noneconomic issues. His reelection argues that ultimately the economy weighed a bit more heavily in the voter's calculus than other issues. The fragile nature of the Truman victory seems captured well by this broader issues model.

Having reviewed the mechanics of prediction, we turn our attention to the surrounding statistics. In the second row, the numbers in parentheses are t-ratios. They tell us whether the coefficients are statistically significant. Here the coefficients of G and PP are both significant at the .05 level, as indicated by the asterisk. (As any t-table in the back of a statistics book would show, to meet this standard for a sample of this particular size, $N = 11$, the absolute value of a t-ratio must exceed 1.86.) Hence, we can safely conclude that it is highly unlikely—less than a 5 in 100 chance—that GNP is actually unrelated to the electoral vote share. Similarly, we can also conclude that popularity is most probably really linked to electoral votes. These significant results suggest that it is, after all, proper to include these two predictor variables in the model.

Below the sample size is the Durbin-Watson (D-W) statistic. Since these eleven elections occur across time, 1948-1988, the Durbin-Watson statistic is worth attending to. It helps assess the degree to which error at one time point is related to error at the next time point. If the D-W value were too high or too low, we could not put much faith in the significance tests we just reported. Fortunately, in this case, the D-W value is close enough to the ideal value of 2.00 that we feel no need to discount the notion that the results are statistically significant.

Next to the Durbin-Watson statistic is the standard error of estimate, SEE. As already discussed, it estimates the expected error from predicting an election that is not in the sample, such as the upcoming election. The SEE for this model is 15.82, substantially less than the SEE of 18.40 for the simple popularity model of equation 2.2. Clearly, incorporating GNP along with popularity can yield more accurate forecasts.

The predictive power of the model is further appreciated by the R-squared (R^2). Practically speaking, it helps assess model performance

Table 3.2 Issues Model: Prediction Error

$$V = -20.90 + 6.83G + 1.40PP$$

Year/incumbent party candidate (party)	(1) Actual electoral vote share	(2) Predicted electoral vote share	(3) Error (1) − (2)	(4) Incumbent party predicted to win or lose	(5) Forecast right or wrong?
1948/Truman (D)	57.1%	50.2%	6.9%	win	right
1952/Stevenson (D)	16.8	24.4	−7.6	lose	right
1956/Eisenhower (R)	86.1	77.5	8.6	win	right
1960/Nixon (R)	40.8	57.4	−16.6	win	wrong
1964/Johnson (D)	90.3	100.0[a]	−9.7	win	right
1968/Humphrey (D)	35.5	54.8	−19.3	win	wrong
1972/Nixon (R)	96.7	86.1	10.6	win	right
1976/Ford (R)	44.6	58.0	−13.4	win	wrong
1980/Carter (D)	9.1	0.0[b]	9.1	lose	right
1984/Reagan (R)	97.6	78.9	18.7	win	right
1988/Bush (R)	79.2	63.6	15.6	win	right

Source: See Appendix.

Notes: R = Republican; D = Democratic. Column 2 is the predicted electoral vote share, according to equation 3.3. On the basis of column 3, average absolute prediction error = 12.37.

[a] In 1964 the model predicted an electoral vote share for Johnson of 103.9. We rounded this to 100.0 since it is not possible to win more than 100.0 percent of the vote.

[b] In 1980 the model predicted a vote share for Carter of −0.9. We rounded this to 0.0 since it is not possible to win less than 0.0 percent of the vote.

(see Lewis-Beck and Skalaban 1990, Achen 1990, and King 1990b for a full treatment of this statistic). The R-squared tells how well the linear regression fits the data. It reports the variation in the predicted variable that can be accounted for by the predictor variables. For our equation, the R-squared of .81 means that GNP and popularity combine to account for 81 percent of the variation in electoral vote share. An R-squared of this magnitude would generally be considered a good fit. Still, there is room for improvement. Specifically, the model fails to account for 19 percent of the variation in the vote.

To get an intuitive sense of the magnitude of the error that remains, look at the predictions on an election-by-election basis. In Table 3.2, we compare the actual electoral vote shares for the president's party with the predictions generated by the model. Column 3 reports the error in prediction for each race. None of the contests is missed by more than 20 percentage points, and in seven of the eleven elections the prediction is off by less than 15 points. This accuracy is summarized in the average absolute prediction error of 12.4. While this is down from the APE of 14.95 for our simple popularity model (Table 2.9), it is still too great.

The large error margin raises the possibility that the model could completely miss a race, declaring a loser to be a winner or vice versa. How well does it do in predicting winners and losers? In order to generate win-lose predictions, the "point" forecasts from our model are transformed by the following rule: if the predicted electoral vote percentage exceeds 50, forecast "win" for the incumbent party; otherwise, forecast "lose." Any model's win-lose forecasting record can be summarized by the outcome error (OE), the proportion of incorrect predictions to total predictions.

Application of the win-lose rule is presented in column 4 of Table 3.2. Column 5 indicates whether or not each prediction was correct. We see that the rule did reasonably well, calling eight of the eleven elections correctly. The corresponding OE is 0.27, figured as follows.

$$\begin{aligned} \text{OE} &= \frac{\text{No. of incorrect win-lose predictions}}{\text{No. of total win-lose predictions}} \\ &= 3/11 \\ &= .27 \end{aligned} \qquad \text{(Eq. 3.4)}$$

This is a respectable score, not that far from no error (OE = .00). Still, it is short of a definitive accounting. Incorporation of other variables, which tap something more than issues, would certainly improve theory and, most likely, predictive power. Now that the basics of multiple regression analysis have been laid out, there are few obstacles in the way of that enterprise.

Issues, Candidates, and Party: A More Complete Model

Our presidential voting theory, despite its simplicity and parsimony, forms an insufficient base for a forecasting model. After all, we know that some presidential voters actually ignore issues when deciding whom to support. Explicit consideration of this group may provide the additional leverage needed to achieve acceptable forecasting accuracy. The research literature on individual vote choice, as already noted, suggests consideration of two other general factors: candidates and party. As for candidates, certain voters choose one candidate over another on the basis of certain physical attributes (such as appearance), moral traits (such as honesty), or values (such as patriotism). Turning to party, some voters depend on their party identification (meaning a psychological attachment to a party) to guide their candidate selection. Overall, these voters tend to set issues aside, relying instead on candidate qualities or party identification.

Can we find macro-level proxies for these micro-level variables? Consider party identification first. The stronger party attachment is in the voting public, the better the party candidates can expect to do in elections. Hence, a sensible measure of party strength might be the national percentage of voters who identify with the incumbent party (Democratic or Republican). Macro-party identification has recently received scholarly attention (see especially MacKuen, Erikson, and Stimson 1989). Unfortunately, when the goal is forecasting, there are several problems with such a measure. First, the availability of preelection data on party loyalties measured with adequate lead time is limited, especially for the early years of the time series. (In particular, Gallup data on party identification at six months prior to the election are not available for 1952 and 1956, even if one relies on the quarter instead of the month.) Further, different polling organizations ask the party identification question in different ways, making it difficult to combine data sources. Third, straight survey measures of party identification are not dynamic and may fail to capture critical changes in the distribution of party support.

To circumvent these difficulties, we decided to use a different, but perhaps more sensitive, indicator of party attachment in the electorate: incumbent party performance in midterm House contests. (Rosenstone [1983, 89-90] uses a similar measure in his presidential election forecasting effort.) The rationale is that this indicator gauges relative party strength heading into the presidential race. A review of history certainly suggests that the notion has merit. For instance, Democratic presidential candidate Humphrey was defeated in 1968, two years after his party had experienced a net loss of a hefty forty-eight seats in the 1966 midterm House elections. Likewise, Ford's 1976 defeat was preceded by a 1974 loss of forty-eight Republican House seats. In contrast, Johnson was swept into the White House in 1964, following his party's relatively good showing in the 1962 House contests. Most recently, Bush captured the presidency after the Republicans did better than expected in the 1986 midterm elections. Although these elections are cited only as examples, they do reflect a general relationship. Incumbent party House seat support at the midterm is actually correlated with electoral vote share, $r = .40$. Thus, it appears to be a party strength indicator of some promise.

Now to the perplexing task of devising a national measure of candidate qualities. With aggregate data, how can individual candidate characteristics such as honesty, integrity, and compassion possibly be measured? The answer is that they cannot be, at least not immediately. Instead, we need to settle for an indirect measure. One indicator of presidential candidate appeal would seem to be their performance in the primaries. The intraparty nature of primaries means that, within them, party identification is of little importance. It also means that issue differences between the primary candidates may be minor. As a result, candidate attributes can dominate primary elections.

If performance in the primaries is a reliable measure of candidate appeal, we should find that the better the candidates do in the primaries, the better they do in the general election. (For a full treatment of the impact of contested primaries on election success, see Wattenberg 1991.) A couple of recent elections provide evidence in support of this hypothesis. In 1980 President Carter faced a stiff challenge in the primaries and went on to lose the general election. Four years later, President Reagan faced no challenger in the primaries and won the general election in a landslide.

For a more formal test of our notion, we calculated the percentage of the total primary vote the incumbent party nominee received in each election from 1948 to 1988. To use our above examples, taking all the primaries together, President Carter won only 51.2 percent of the votes cast, in contrast to President Reagan's 98.6 percent. In general, when this primary variable is calculated for each incumbent candidate (1948-1988) and correlated with electoral vote success, we find $r = .52$. This strong correlation encourages a further simplification, to make the variable more useful for forecasting. That is, we divide the variable values into strong candidates (those who receive at least 60 percent of the total primary vote) and weak candidates (who receive less than 60 percent). This dichotomous variable (scored 1 and 0, respectively) correlates even more strongly with electoral success, $r = .60$.

We are now ready to incorporate our new party strength (PS) and candidate appeal (C) variables into a more fully, and more properly, specified presidential election model. In words, we might write

$$\text{Electoral vote} = \text{Economic conditions} + \text{Presidential popularity} + \text{Party strength} + \text{Candidate appeal} \qquad \text{(Eq. 3.5)}$$

These two new variables, PS and C, along with the previous GNP and popularity measures, are included in the following multiple regression equation:

$$\begin{array}{l} V = 6.83 + 7.76{*}G + 0.86{*}PP + 0.52{*}PS + 19.66{*}C \\ \quad\;\; (0.50) \quad (3.79) \quad\quad (3.39) \quad\quad (2.87) \quad\quad (3.30) \end{array}$$

$R^2 = .95$ Adj. $R^2 = .92$ $N = 11$
SEE = 9.10 D-W = 2.34

where V, G, and PP are defined as in equation 3.3; PS = number of House seats incumbent party lost in last midterm election; C = percentage of total primary vote incumbent party candidate received, scored 1 if the nominee received at least 60 percent of the vote, 0 if the nominee received less than 60 percent; * = statistically significant at

.05, one-tail, $|t| > 1.94$; adj. R^2 = coefficient of multiple determination adjusted for the small number of cases; all other terms as equation 3.3.

The evidence of equation 3.5 strongly supports our revised theory. All the predictor variables have statistically significant coefficients, which suggests that they are properly placed in the model. (Note that the .05 level results are based on a one-tail test, actually more appropriate since our hypotheses about the coefficients all have one direction; that is, an increase in any of the variables is expected to increase incumbent support.) Further, the estimated effects seem quite plausible, according to the respective coefficients. For every percentage increase in GNP, the president's party can expect an extra 7.76 percentage share of the electoral vote. When the president's popularity rises 1 point, the incumbent candidate should net almost 1 percent more (that is, .86) of the electoral vote. If the candidate was strong in the primaries, he or she will likely post a gain of just under 20 percentage points (more precisely, 19.66). Finally, the incumbent party can plan on 1 percent more of the electoral vote for every two House seats it avoided losing at the midterm (that is, $2.0 \times .52 = 1.04$).

These effects are interesting on their own, and they certainly lend credence to the theory they mirror. However, what most intrigues us, as forecasters, are the summary statistics on model performance. First, the R-squared of .95 is extremely high, indicating that only 5 percent of the variation in electoral vote share is left unaccounted for. (Moreover, it remains extremely high, at .92, even when it is adjusted to take into account the small sample size relative to the number of predictor variables.) Further, the SEE is just 9.10, well below the 15.82 of the less complete issues model of equation 3.3.

How well does our new model predict actual winners and losers from contest to contest? The answer is displayed in Table 3.3. Our win-lose forecasts for every contest are in column 4. To generate these we used the same criterion as we did in Table 3.2: if the predicted electoral vote percentage (column 2) is greater than 50, the incumbent party candidate will win; if not, the candidate will lose. A check of column 5 indicates correct predictions of the outcome in all but one race (for an OE = .09). The sole miss was 1960, when the model forecasted a narrow Nixon victory. Instead, Kennedy prevailed on election day in one of the closest presidential contests in history, a race so tight it was impossible to forecast.

The average absolute prediction error is only 5.63, less than half the size of the APE for the issues model (equation 3.3). An electoral vote shift of this size is equivalent to a popular vote shift of something over 1 percent.[1] How good is this performance? As a baseline of comparison, consider again the final preelection day Gallup polls (see Table 1.3). After conducting that poll, Gallup usually tries to allocate the undecided voters, in order to make a point estimate of the actual popular vote

Table 3.3 Full Presidential Model: Prediction Error

$$V = 6.83 + 7.76G + 0.86PP + 0.52PS + 19.66C$$

Year/incumbent party candidate (party)	(1) Actual electoral vote share	(2) Predicted electoral vote share	(3) Error (1) − (2)	(4) Incumbent party predicted to win or lose	(5) Forecast right or wrong?
1948/Truman (D)	57.1%	51.0%	6.1%	win	right
1952/Stevenson (D)	16.8	20.0	−3.2	lose	right
1956/Eisenhower (R)	86.1	78.9	7.2	win	right
1960/Nixon (R)	40.8	55.6	−14.8	win	wrong
1964/Johnson (D)	90.3	92.4	−2.1	win	right
1968/Humphrey (D)	35.5	38.9	−3.4	lose	right
1972/Nixon (R)	96.7	100.0[a]	−3.3	win	right
1976/Ford (R)	44.6	39.0	5.6	lose	right
1980/Carter (D)	9.1	6.0	3.1	lose	right
1984/Reagan (R)	97.6	88.1	9.5	win	right
1988/Bush (R)	79.2	82.8	3.6	win	right

Source: See Appendix.

Notes: R = Republican; D = Democratic. Column 2 is the predicted electoral vote share, according to equation 3.5. On the basis of column 3, average absolute prediction error = 5.63.

[a]In 1972 the model predicted an electoral vote share for Nixon of 101.1. We rounded this to 100.0 since it is not possible to win more than 100.0 percent of the vote.

percentages. By this method, the error in their popular vote estimate for the incumbent candidate (1948-1988) is about 2.2 percent (*Gallup Reports*). In other words, these Gallup estimates, based on day-before data, yield about twice the error of this forecasting model, which is based on predictor variables measured the summer before the election.

As powerful as the model appears, it must be recognized that its construction has occurred after the fact. All the elections under study (1948-1988) have, obviously, already taken place. The predictions in Table 3.3, then, were calculated by relating known scores on the predictor variables with known electoral vote scores. Have we simply lucked into a combination of elections that happen to fit this model extremely well? Perhaps, with a different sample, the predictions would be much less accurate.

To test for this possibility, we estimated our full presidential equation using various sets of elections. Table 3.4 displays the results, reestimating the model after dropping different years. The R-squared and the standard error of estimate are reported for the full sample from 1948 to 1988 (row 1). The same statistics are calculated again, but for a

Table 3.4 Predictive Stability of the Full Presidential Model

(1) Sample of elections	(2) Sample size (N)	(3) R^2	(4) Standard error of estimate (SEE)
1948-1988	11	.95	9.1
1948-1984	10	.95	9.8
1948-1980	9	.96	9.6
1948-1976	8	.94	10.9
1948-1972	7	.95	12.2
Random	7	.99	4.3

Note: Column 1 lists the elections included in each sample. In each row, the full presidential model of equation 3.5 is reestimated on a different sample.

reduced sample from 1948 to 1984 (row 2). Once more, the fit statistics are estimated for a further reduced sample from 1948 to 1980. We continue this process until almost half the elections are eliminated (and the number of independent variables almost equals the number of cases). Finally, using a random number table, we randomly eliminated four cases, leaving a sample of only seven elections (the last row).

These tests demonstrate that the model has considerable stability. The R-squared remains virtually unchanged, and the SEE remains low (rising only slightly as the sample size becomes perilously small). Overall, then, the results of the model from the full sample are more than luck. Instead, they seem to reflect the actual structure of aggregate relationships in the modern world of presidential elections.

Conclusion

Presidential election outcomes are shaped by different forces. In this chapter, we explored three types: issues, party strength, and candidate appeal. We attempted to measure these forces at the national level and to incorporate them into a properly specified regression equation. The results are satisfying in several respects. For one, the model is theoretically attractive; that is, it includes proxy variables representing major explanations of individual vote choice in presidential contests. More important for our purposes, though, the model produces accurate predictions. Across the eleven elections under study, the model generates fairly precise electoral vote share estimates, calling the winner correctly ten times. This precision is doubly encouraging, given that each forecast is produced with data available in the summer before the election. It does not seem out of the question to suppose that the model could serve well in forecasting future elections. In Chapter 9, we apply the model to the upcoming (1992) presidential contest. Before that, however, we will explore forecasting possibilities in other electoral arenas. We begin with the House of Representatives.

Note

1. When electoral vote share is regressed on popular vote share (1948-1988), the results are as follows:

$$\text{Electoral vote} = -160.5 + 4.27(\text{popular vote})$$

   We observe that an increase of about 1.3 percent in the popular vote would be expected to produce a 5.6 percent shift in the electoral vote (i.e., $1.31 \times 4.27 = 5.6$).

CHAPTER 4

House Elections

Every president enters the White House pledged to implement a set of policies spoken about during the campaign. These program goals are often bundled together under catchy vote-getting phrases, such as Franklin Roosevelt's New Deal, Lyndon Johnson's Great Society, and Ronald Reagan's New Beginning. Whatever the name, these policies promise to take the nation in a different direction. However, just because a president articulates plans does not mean they will be accomplished. Implementation requires the support of numerous political institutions, not the least of which is Congress. Without sufficient backing from the legislature, a chief executive's agenda faces rough sledding.

Some presidents enjoy a cooperative House and Senate, with members voting in favor of almost every initiative coming from the Oval Office. For example, much of FDR's early New Deal legislation passed through Congress without a hitch. It helped, of course, that Roosevelt carried into office on his coattails a heavily Democratic legislature. Lyndon Johnson was another president who was able to persuade Congress to endorse most of his agenda. His landslide victory of 1964, coupled with extensive Democratic gains in the House and Senate, laid the groundwork for the passage of his Great Society programs—the War on Poverty, Medicare, the Voting Rights Act, to name a few. By way of contrast, his successor, Richard Nixon, had much of his social agenda—mostly aimed at undoing Johnson's welfare legislation—succumb to a Democratic-dominated Congress. When he took office in 1968, for instance, Republicans controlled only 44 percent of the House seats and 43 percent of the Senate seats.

Congressional scholar Gary Jacobson (1983, 132) summarizes this

Table 4.1 Presidential Success and Partisan Balance in the House

President	Presidential success[a]	Proportion controlled by the president's party: House	Senate
Eisenhower	72.2%	44.8%	45.8%
Kennedy	85.4	60.0	66.0
Johnson	81.5	62.5	66.0
Nixon	67.0	43.0	43.0
Ford	57.4	33.0	37.0
Carter	76.5	65.0	59.5
Reagan	61.9	41.3	51.3

[a]Presidential success percentages are figured from the *Congressional Quarterly Almanac* (1989) annual percentages of "presidential victories on congressional votes on which the president took a clear position."

link between a president's success in Congress and the partisan makeup of the legislature as follows: "Sheer numbers matter; administrations get more of what they want from Congress the more seats their party holds in the House and Senate." Support for Jacobson's contention appears in Table 4.1, comparing the party balance in the House and Senate with the percentage of the president's proposed policies that Congress passed. Presidents like Johnson and Carter, who had many partisan allies in Congress, managed to pass much more of their legislation than presidents like Nixon and Ford, who faced assemblies dominated by the other party.

Obviously, Congress is a major player in the national policy arena. Legislators can, and often do, act as a check on presidential proposals, just as our nation's founders envisioned. In light of the agenda-shaping powers of Congress, it becomes important to understand the forces that determine the outcome of legislative elections. This chapter and the next attempt to do so. Beginning with the House, we offer a brief discussion of how to measure election outcomes in the lower chamber. Then we develop an explanation for those outcomes. Finally, we examine the forecasting potential of that explanation.

Measuring House Election Outcomes

Inertia is a very important factor in election contests for the House. Representatives running for reelection almost always win. For example, in 1988, 98 percent of the members seeking another term were victorious (401 out of 408). Taking a broader perspective, since 1950 more than 93

Table 4.2 Partisan Composition and Seat Change in the House, 1946-1990

Election (president's party)	Partisan composition		Net seat gain or loss for president's party
	Democrats	Republicans	
1946 (D)	188	245	—
1948 (D)	263	171	75
1950 (D)	234	199	−29[a]
1952 (D)	211	221	−23
1954 (R)	232	203	−18[a]
1956 (R)	233	200	−3
1958 (R)	283	153	−47[a]
1960 (R)	263	174	21
1962 (D)	258	177	−5[a]
1964 (D)	295	140	37
1966 (D)	247	187	−48[a]
1968 (D)	243	192	−4
1970 (R)	254	180	−12[a]
1972 (R)	239	192	12
1974 (R)	291	144	−48[a]
1976 (R)	292	143	−1
1978 (D)	276	157	−16[a]
1980 (D)	243	192	−33
1982 (R)	269	165	−27[a]
1984 (R)	252	182	17
1986 (R)	258	177	−5[a]
1988 (R)	260	175	−2
1990 (R)	267	167	−8[a]

Note: R = Republican; D = Democratic.

[a]Midterm elections.

percent of the incumbents trying to hold their seats succeeded. Despite this stability, reelection is not automatic. In a typical election year, 30 or so incumbents lose and another 30 to 40 members decide not to seek reelection. Sometimes, substantial shifts in the partisan composition of the House have taken place. At one extreme, in 1948 the Democrats picked up 75 seats. At the other extreme, the Democrats experienced a net loss of 48 seats in 1966. Table 4.2 presents a history of partisan variation in the House from 1946 to 1990.

Party composition of the House (Democratic versus Republican seats) is listed, along with the political party of the president. Furthermore, what these shifts amount to, in terms of the overall gain or loss for the president's party, appears in the last column. Clearly, incumbent fortunes vary from contest to contest, and the pattern is not random. For one, the president's party usually experiences a net seat loss, as indicated by negative scores in seventeen of the twenty-two elections. Indeed, averaging the entire seat change series, we calculate that any presidential administration can expect to lose about 8 seats overall. Thus, it costs something to govern. The electorate, acting collectively, seems to punish incumbents for serving by voting against them. Further, they punish them more at certain times than at others. Look at the seat change scores marked with the letter "a," indicating that they occurred between the presidential election years, at midterm. It is in these midterm contests that the heaviest loses are encountered, with an average incumbent drop of about 24 seats. Moreover, a gain was not posted in even one of these contests, a condition that has prevailed since 1934. Why do presidents and their party routinely have to pay such a price for governing? What circumstances generate the instances of party benefits for the president in House races? We consider these issues in the next section.

House Election Outcomes: A Conventional Explanation

Among politicians, a common notion is that voters in House contests cast ballots primarily on the basis of national questions. In particular, voters are held to focus on how well the president is handling important issues. If, for instance, a Republican is president and voters are pleased with the president's performance, they will respond by supporting Republican candidates in House races. But if the president's performance is viewed as inadequate, they will vote for Democratic candidates. This perspective is nicely summed up by Edward Tufte (1978, 106): "Overall election outcomes represent a referendum on the incumbent administration's handling of the economy and of other issues." This describes an equation very similar to our issues model for presidential elections:

$$\text{Election outcome} = \text{Economic} + \text{Noneconomic issues} \qquad \text{(Eq. 4.1)}$$

Do individual citizens in congressional elections evaluate the national economy, then reward or punish the incumbent accordingly, much as they do in presidential contests? Considerable survey research has been carried out on this question. What the studies suggest is that evaluations regarding the whole economy almost always have an impact on the congressional vote. In an extensive investigation, D. Roderick Kiewiet (1983, 102-107) found that economic bad times cost the incumbent party votes. More precisely, assessments of national economic conditions had a statistically significant effect in nine of the twelve House elections from 1958 through 1980. However, in common with other studies, the particular economic

Figure 4.1 The Relationship Between Collective Economic Evaluations and the Vote

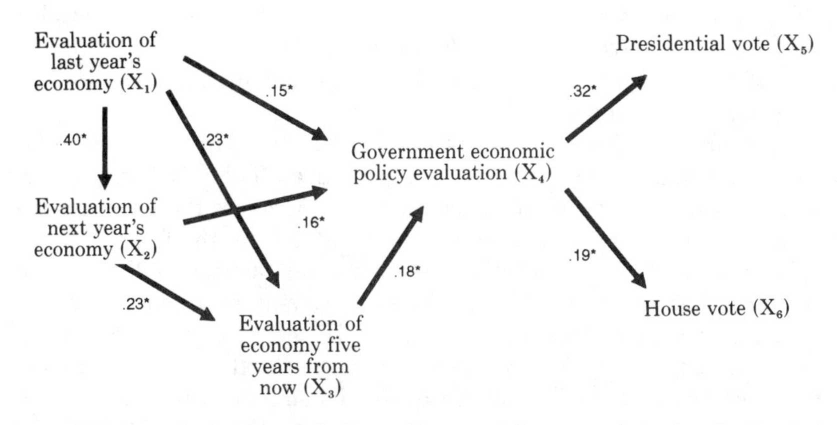

Source: Michigan Survey Research Center Surveys of Consumer Attitudes, January 1984.
Notes: The estimates are from multiple regression (standardized coefficients); the asterisk indicates statistical significance at .05; N = 521. Not pictured are the paths from the control variables (income, gender, race, party identification).

conditions that triggered the vote varied; that is, sometimes the primary factor was inflation, sometimes unemployment, sometimes general business conditions (see also Jacobson 1989, 773-774).

The basic point is that overall evaluations of the economy influence congressional vote choice. The specific mechanisms of this micro-linkage are not our immediate concern, since we wish to account for macro-election outcomes. Still, it is worth briefly offering one version of that linkage, as sketched in Figure 4.1 (see Lewis-Beck 1988b, 131-133). The statistical estimates in the figure come from a 1984 election survey. They argue that a voter's assessment of the economy (that is, past and future business conditions) clearly shapes his or her evaluation of the administration's handling of economic policy. In turn, that economic policy evaluation significantly influences the House vote intention, as well as the presidential vote intention.

The significant effects of these global economic evaluations on congressional vote choice imply that in seeking proxy measures for our national forecasting model we should focus on the more inclusive aggregate indicators, as we did in the presidential case. The macroeconomic indicators of unemployment, inflation, income, and GNP are well correlated with each other (recall Table 3.1), so we can infer that they measure much the same thing. However, two seem conceptually more general—real disposable income and GNP growth. Which should we choose?

In the presidential model of Chapter 3, we selected GNP. A glance at relevant published presidential models shows that, of those that use an economy variable, half use a GNP measure and half use an income measure (see Table 6.1). In contrast, almost all the relevant congressional models in the literature measure the economy with an income variable. (This tradition took root from Kramer [1971] and Tufte [1975]; the relevant congressional models, as well as the presidential models, are fully compared in Chapter 6.)

How much difference does choosing one measure over the other make? In a quantitative sense, not a great deal. The GNP and income measures are very similar empirically ($r = .75$, across these twenty-two House election years, measured as growth rates from the fourth quarter of the year prior to the election to the second quarter of the election year). Further, each correlates moderately well with our dependent variable of House seat change. For the GNP measure, $r = .35$; for the income measure, $r = .59$. To follow the fixed precedent of past congressional research, we will emphasize the income measure over GNP. However, for comparison's sake we also report the model below with GNP substituted as the economic indicator.

The relationship between seat change and real disposable income is displayed graphically in Figure 4.2. The firm connection is obvious, and it would be more so without the outlying observation in the lower right-hand corner. The "outlier" comes from 1950, when President Harry Truman and the Democrats lost 29 seats, despite a surging economy. This apparent anomaly is informative, for it reminds us of the role of noneconomic issues. During that summer, Truman's Gallup approval rating was exceedingly low, registering only 37 percent in June. Besides confronting an electorate deeply dissatisfied with Truman over noneconomic issues, the House Democrats also faced a midterm contest, with its historic pattern of incumbent losses.

When these extra circumstances—low popularity and midterm time—are taken into account, the outlier status of the 1950 result is less surprising. Moreover, they show us that an adequate explanatory model of House election outcomes should include measures that tap noneconomic issues, such as presidential popularity. A properly specified model should also somehow adjust results for the inevitable effects of the electoral calendar, namely whether the election occurs at midterm. We might summarize this fairly conventional model as follows:

$$\begin{matrix}\text{House} \\ \text{seat} \\ \text{change}\end{matrix} = \begin{matrix}\text{Economic} \\ \text{conditions}\end{matrix} + \begin{matrix}\text{Presidential} \\ \text{popularity}\end{matrix} + \text{Midterm status} \qquad \text{(Eq. 4.2)}$$

Predicting the dependent variable of incumbent House seat change (HC) from the independent variables of income growth (the economic variable,

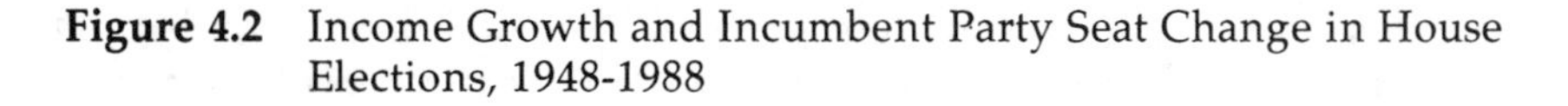

Figure 4.2 Income Growth and Incumbent Party Seat Change in House Elections, 1948-1988

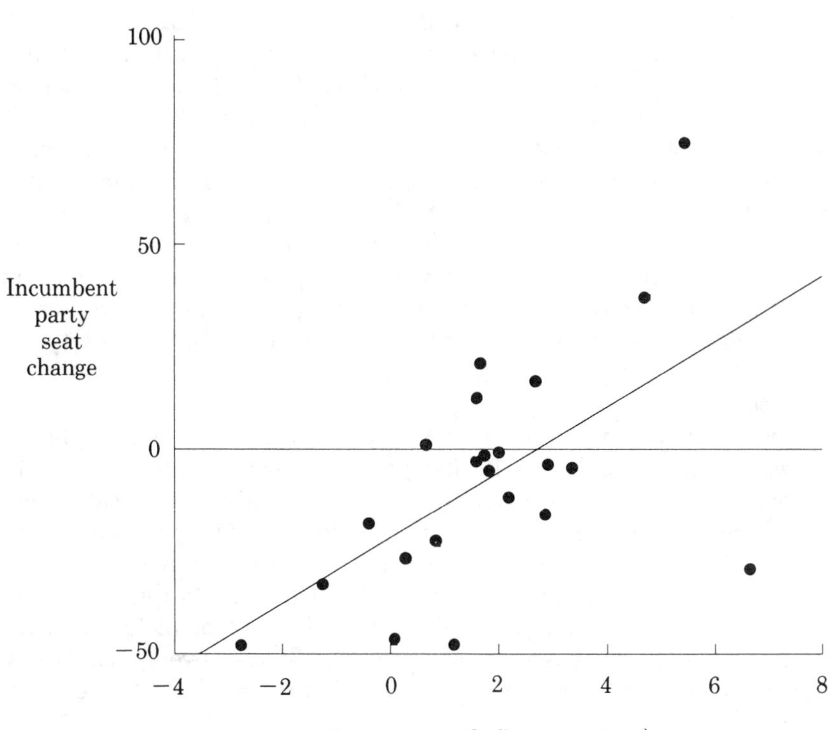

Note: Income growth is the change from the fourth quarter in the year before the election to the second quarter of the election year.

E), presidential popularity (PP), and midterm status (M) yields the following regression estimates[1]:

$$HC = \underset{(-3.98)}{-63.75*} + \underset{(3.21)}{6.20*E} + \underset{(2.01)}{0.60*PP} + \underset{(3.68)}{29.08*M}$$

$R^2 = .66$ Adj. $R^2 = .60$ $N = 22$
SEE = 18.13 D-W = 1.96

where HC = number of seats gained or lost by the president's party; E = growth rate of real disposable income six months before the election (the change from the fourth quarter in the year before the election to the second quarter of the election year); PP = percent approving of the president's job handling in the June Gallup poll of the election year; M = a dichotomous variable for midterm election (scored 0) or presidential year election (scored 1); the figures in parentheses are t-ratios; * = statistically significant at .05 or more, one-tail, $|t| > 1.73$; the remaining statistics are defined as with equation 3.5.

This explanation for House seat change is good as far as it goes. It is similar in form to our previously published House forecasting models, which performed rather well at the time (Lewis-Beck 1987; Lewis-Beck and Rice 1984, 1988). Also, the significant coefficients suggest plausible effects. First, the slope of 6.20 for the economy variable indicates that with a 1 percent growth increase, the incumbent party can expect to gain an extra 6 seats. Second, the popularity coefficient of .60 implies that when the president's approval rating jumps 2 points, his party can count on at least 1 more seat in Congress. Third, barring any positive impact from these economic and popularity variables, the president's party can anticipate losing about 29 seats in a midterm race (on the basis of the M coefficient).

Substantively, then, the model makes some sense. However, the big drawback for our purposes is that prediction error is great. First, the R-squared indicates that about one-third of the variation in seat change is left unexplained. The extent of the implied error is quantified in the SEE, which registers more than 18 seats. Perhaps the magnitude of the error is caused by incomplete specification of the model. Certain important independent variables may have been left out or included in the wrong way, as recent literature has suggested. This conventional, issues-based explanation of seat change in the House seems ripe for revision.

Revising the Model: Midterms, the Economy, Risk

A recent debate on aggregate House election outcomes hints that the importance of the economic effect has been exaggerated, or perhaps the effect is confined to midterm elections (Erikson 1990; Jacobson 1990). Does the impact of macroeconomics depend on whether the election year is or is not a presidential year? The scatterplots of Figure 4.3 speak directly to this question. Income growth is again related to seat change, first for presidential years, then for midterm years.

The results are intriguing. In both plots the relationship is positive, indicating that an improved economy tends to benefit the incumbent party. However, the *strength* of that relationship depends considerably on election type. For presidential years the correlation between income growth and seat change is r = .89; for midterms it is r = .38. Further, the slope predicts that a 1 percent income change will produce a 14-seat change in presidential years, in contrast to a 3-seat change in midterm years.

Figure 4.3 Income Growth and Incumbent Party Seat Change in House Elections in Presidential and Midterm Election Years, 1948-1990

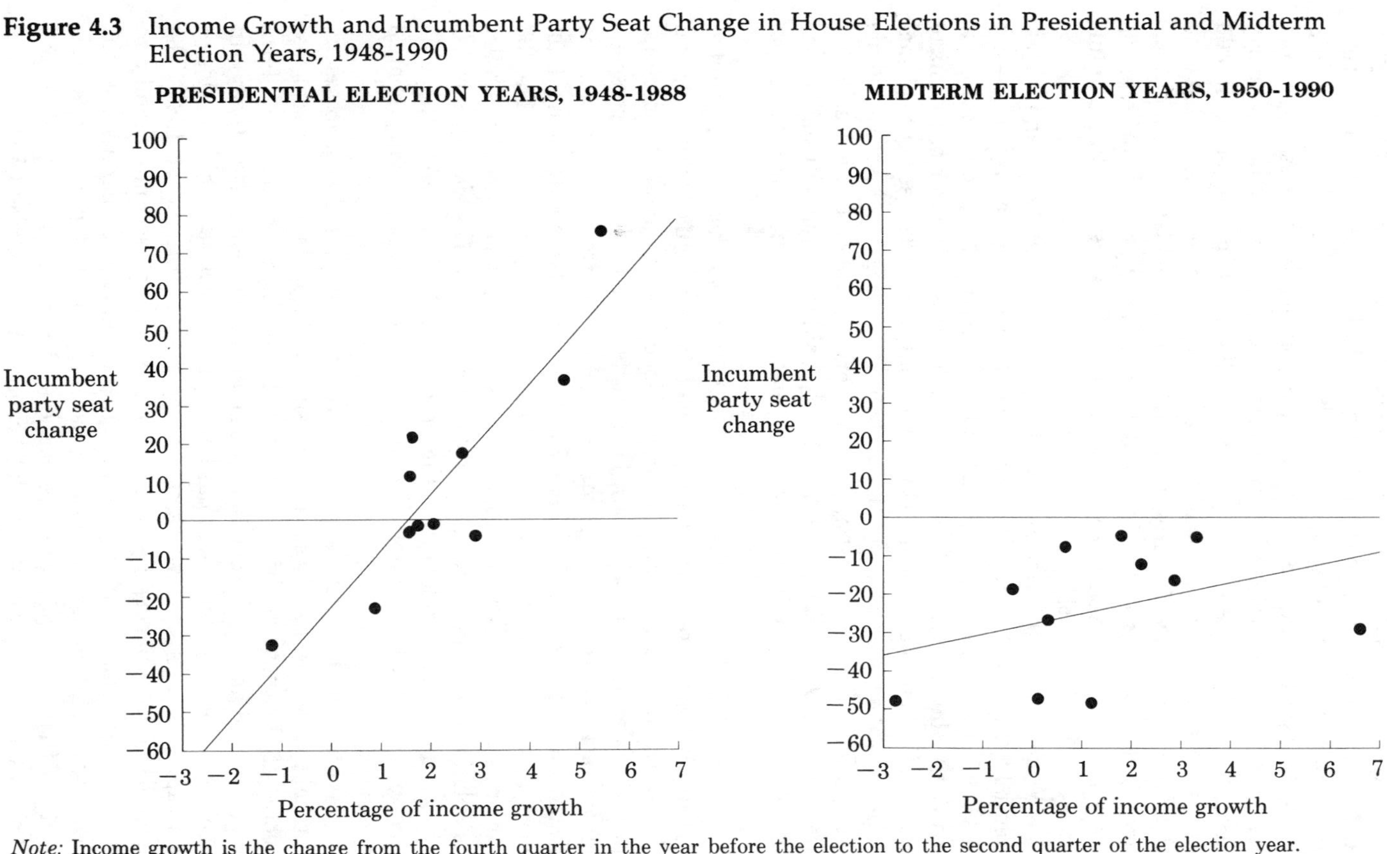

Note: Income growth is the change from the fourth quarter in the year before the election to the second quarter of the election year.

According to these results congressional voters are, after all, responsive to macroeconomic changes. However, and what is most interesting, they are more responsive for contests held at presidential election time. Reflecting on the individual voter's decision-making process, this does not seem unreasonable. We know voters reward the incumbent party according to how the economy performs. Thus, economic issues should carry more weight in on-year House races, when voters also have on their minds a choice for president, the country's chief economic manager. But regardless of the individual choice mechanism involved, it is clear that these on-year/off-year economic differences need to be built into our macro-model.

What other differences are there between midterm and presidential year elections? We have mentioned that it is hard—not to say impossible—for the president's party to avoid net seat losses at the midterm. What is in the nature of midterms to make that so? A simple reason, which has only recently received formal consideration, is that the incumbent is going against the odds (see Oppenheimer, Stimson, and Waterman 1986; Lewis-Beck and Rice 1985). At midterm time, the president's party usually has more seats up than in the previous election, so the party risks losing more.

The vulnerability of these extra incumbent seats has been accounted for by the exposure thesis (see especially Oppenheimer, Stimson, and Waterman 1986). First, take Democratic incumbents. Across the electoral period under study (1948-1990), Democrats have held 257 House seats, on average. However, going into the 1966 midterm, for example, the Democrats held 295 seats. That is, they had 38 more seats up than normal, in terms of the historic average (295 − 257 = 38). This 38 indicates the number of "exposed" seats the party had. A similar calculation can be made for Republican incumbents. The average number of Republican seat holders for the period is 177. But, before the 1958 midterm contest, for example, Republicans held 200 seats, giving them 23 exposed seats.

With such high levels of exposure, the heavy midterm losses by incumbents would hardly seem surprising. Indeed, the heaviest seat loss scores of this postwar period occurred in the highly exposed midterm races of 1958 and 1966 (that is, losses of 48 and 47 seats, respectively). In contrast, when the incumbent has few seats exposed, then midterm losses can appear curiously low. Consider the recent example of 1986. The incumbent Republicans lost a total of only 5 seats, seeming thereby to defy midterm history and perhaps signal a partisan realignment of the electorate. This apparent curiosity is easily accounted for, once it is realized that the exposure score was only 5 (that is, 182 − 177 = 5). Put another way, going into the 1986 contest, the incumbent Republicans

Table 4.3 The Number of Exposed Seats for the President's Party: House Elections, 1948-1990

Election (president's party)	Number of seats exposed	Election (president's party)	Number of seats exposed
1948 (D)	−69	1970 (R)	15[a]
1950 (D)	6[a]	1972 (R)	3
1952 (D)	−23	1974 (R)	15[a]
1954 (R)	44[a]	1976 (R)	−33
1956 (R)	26	1978 (D)	35[a]
1958 (R)	23[a]	1980 (D)	19
1960 (R)	−24	1982 (R)	15[a]
1962 (D)	6[a]	1984 (R)	−12
1964 (D)	1	1986 (R)	5[a]
1966 (D)	38[a]	1988 (R)	0
1968 (D)	−10	1990 (R)	−2[a]

Notes: For the president's party, R = Republican, D = Democratic. To calculate the number of seats exposed the average number of House seats the president's party has held over the 1948-1990 period was figured (for Democrats the average held was 257, for Republicans the average was 177). Next, the average number of seats held was subtracted from the number of seats the president's party held going into each election. For example, going into the 1966 election, the Democratic party was incumbent and it held 295 seats. Thus, the Democrats had 38 seats exposed (295 − 257 = 38).

[a]Midterm elections.

were already at a relatively low level, so they were unlikely to lose many more seats.

For each election, midterm and presidential, we calculated a seat exposure score for the incumbent party, arriving at the results of Table 4.3. Taking all eleven midterms together, the average number of seats exposed is 18.2. Clearly, at midterm time the president's party generally has extra seats on the line. Other things being equal, then, the losses will inevitably be greater. Conversely, in presidential election years the incumbent party is actually underexposed in terms of vulnerable seats. Averaging the exposure scores for the eleven presidential years yields a negative value, −11.1. Without doubt, the incumbent party runs a bigger risk of seat loss in midterm years.

Overall, this exposure variable correlates well with whether the election is at midterm or not, generating an $r = -.61$. Moreover, exposure correlates highly ($r = -.71$) with seat change, the variable we want to forecast. The more seats the incumbent party has exposed, the more seats it is likely to lose. These strong findings on incumbent "seats exposed" definitely bear incorporation into a fuller model of congressional election outcomes. But before we present one, we need to consider incumbent long-run risk.

The question of exposure and midterm loss highlights a larger problem: the electoral cost of governing (see also Paldam 1986). A broad implication is that the longer the president is in office, the more opposition may gather among congressional voters, who seek to blame someone for accumulated woes. Such a phenomenon certainly can occur with the president's popularity itself as it begins to decline, occasionally notoriously, after the initial "honeymoon" period. As John Mueller (1973) observed, over time a "coalition of minorities" who are dissatisfied forms against the president. Perhaps, then, in the long run incumbency works against itself with respect to House strength.

Over the long haul, does the president's congressional backing erode, as measured in the number of seats the party is able to hold? There is some evidence that this is so. The biggest losses incumbent parties experienced across this series occurred in 1958, 1966, and 1974—years in which the president's party had served for six years. All these races were midterms after the president's party had been reelected to the White House. Thus they might be called second midterms. Incumbent losses for second midterms average −37 seats, more than double the losses (at −15.6) for the first midterms of a new president. Moreover, this drop in support over time may extend beyond second midterms. For example, by 1988 the Republicans had held presidential office for eight years. They experienced a net loss of House seats in that year, although it was a presidential year in which they were incumbent. These examples suggest a general negative trend from incumbency tenure that is worth testing.

House Seat Change: A Less Conventional Explanation

We have moved away from our more conventional explanation of House seat change (in equation 4.2). The issue variables remain as core determinants. However, at least with regard to economic issues, they appear to operate differently depending on whether the election is a midterm. Further, the level of incumbent risk seems to have an important impact. In particular, it is critical to ask how exposed the president's party is in terms of the number of seats it has up. Beyond that, as the party's time in the White House extends across terms, its congressional strength apparently tends to diminish.

Taking these points into account, we offer a revised explanation for incumbent seat change, as sketched in Figure 4.4. The variables of the conventional model—income growth and presidential popularity—still occupy center stage. However, the effect of income growth is an interaction, operating at one strength in a midterm election, another in a presidential year. Furthermore, our two new risk variables—seats ex-

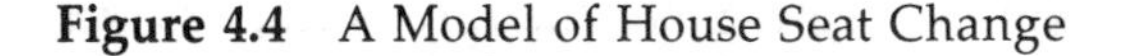

Figure 4.4 A Model of House Seat Change

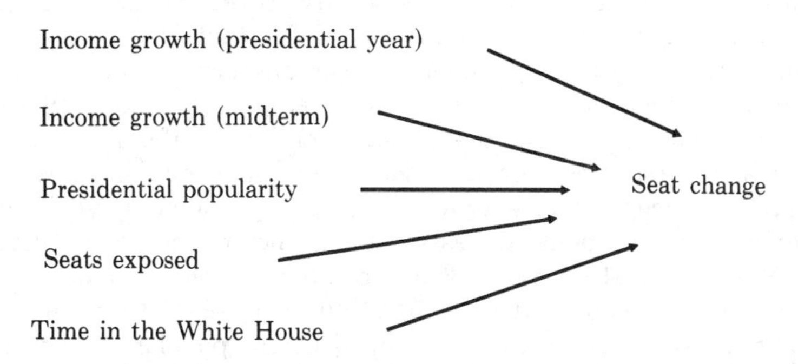

posed and time in office—are presumed to have their own impact. (Of course, other specifications could be considered. The model below actually captures party identification and candidate appeal, familiar variables from the presidential model.[2])

The formulation suggested in Figure 4.4 holds up rather well, when estimated in the following multiple regression equation[3]:

$$HC = -24.43* + 1.70^{a}E + 7.54*(E \times M) + 0.53*PP - 0.65*X - 7.14*T \quad \text{(Eq. 4.3)}$$

$$(-1.95) \quad (1.31) \quad (3.55) \quad (2.86) \quad (-4.32) \quad (-2.93)$$

$R^2 = .90$ Adj. $R^2 = .87$ $N = 22$
SEE = 10.30 D-W = 2.17

where variables HC, E, PP, and M are measured as in equation 4.2; variable (E × M) = the multiplication of the E and M variables, allowing income to have extra weight during the presidential years; X = the number of seats the president's party has exposed, as measured in Table 4.3; T = length of time the president's party has been in the White House (1 = first midterm election after a change in party control of the presidency, for 1954, 1962, 1970, 1978, and 1982; 2 = year of a party's first reelection bid, for 1956, 1964, 1972, 1980, and 1984; 3 = midterm election year after a party has won the presidency for the second time, for 1958, 1966, 1974, and 1986; 4 = election years when the party has controlled the presidency for two or more terms, for 1948, 1950, 1952, 1960, 1968, 1976, 1988, and 1990); * = statistically significant at .05 or better, $|t| > 1.75$; [a] = not quite statistically significant at .10 ($|t| > 1.34$); all the other terms are defined as in equation 4.2.

Before we examine the forecasting accuracy of the model, we should interpret the coefficients. With regard to the economy, the incumbent party can count on about 2 extra seats for every 1 percent growth in income if it is a midterm year. (Since the E coefficient misses statistical significance at .10 by only three-hundredths of a point according to the t-ratio, we feel it prudent to stick with this interpretation.) For a presidential year, another 7 or 8 seats should be added to that number, for a total net gain of about 10 seats. Economic boom or bust, then, can spell the difference between a good and a bad year for the incumbent party in the House. For instance, 4 percent income growth during a presidential year would probably generate about 37 seats for the incumbent party [that is, (1.70 × 4) + (7.54 × 4) = 36.96], compared with a gain of no seats if income growth is 0 [that is, (1.70 × 0) + (7.54 × 0) = .00].

The impact of other issues is tapped by the popularity coefficient. Accordingly, every drop of 2 percentage points in a president's popularity translates into a loss of approximately 1 incumbent seat in the House (.53 × 2 = 1.06). Clearly, party fortunes in the House are significantly influenced by the president's standing with the voters. For example, a president with relatively higher ratings, say 60 percent, could count on about 11 more seats than a president with low popularity, say 40 percent [(60 − 40 = 20) × .53 = 10.6].

Thus, the trio of variables in the conventional House model—income, popularity, and election type—continue to be important predictors of seat change. But the strong statistical significance of the two new additions to the model, exposure and White House tenure, indicate that the original variables tell only part of the story. The coefficient for exposure (X) suggests that for every 2 seats the incumbent party has exposed, it can expect to lose at least 1 (.65 × 2 = 1.30). Suppose in a midterm election 20 incumbent seats were exposed. The president's party could anticipate losing about 13 of these seats (.65 × 20 = 13.0). The exposure idea continues to appear to be the key to solving the midterm loss puzzle.

Last, the coefficient for the trend variable T implies that the longer a party stays in the Oval Office, the more its partisan strength in the House will fail. The magnitude of this decay is imposing, about 7 seats every two years. As an example, from a party's first midterm (two years after partisan control of the White House changes) to its second midterm four years later (two years after the party has been reelected to the presidency), it can expect to control about 14 fewer seats in the House.

Taken together, the coefficients present a comprehensive picture of the forces that shape the partisan makeup of the House. From the perspective of statistical inference, it is comforting that they settle near conventional levels of significance or beyond. But the fundamental question remains: How well do these measures combine to predict seat change?

Table 4.4 Forecasting Accuracy of the House Model

$$HC = -24.43 + 1.70E + 7.54E \times M + 0.53PP - 0.65X - 7.14T$$

Year (president's party)	(1) Actual seat change	(2) Predicted seat change	(3) Error (1) − (2)	(4) Forecast good or bad year?	(5) Forecast right or wrong?
1948 (D)	75	63	11	good	right
1950 (D)	−29	−26	—	bad	right
1952 (D)	−23	−13	−10	bad	right
1954 (R)	−18	−28	1	bad	wrong
1956 (R)	−3	−4	1	bad	right
1958 (R)	−47	−32	−15	bad	right
1960 (R)	21	10	11	good	right
1962 (D)	−5	5	−10	good	right
1964 (D)	37	44	−7	good	right
1966 (D)	−48	−43	—	bad	right
1968 (D)	−4	2	−6	good	wrong
1970 (R)	−12	−8	−4	good	right
1972 (R)	12	4	8	good	right
1974 (R)	−48	−47	−1	bad	right
1976 (R)	−1	11	−12	good	wrong
1978 (D)	−16	−27	11	bad	wrong
1980 (D)	−33	−46	13	bad	right
1982 (R)	−27	−17	−10	good	wrong
1984 (R)	17	21	−4	good	right
1986 (R)	−5	−11	6	good	right
1988 (R)	−2	−10	8	bad	right
1990 (R)	−8	−15	7	good	right

Notes: For presidential election years a good year is when the incumbent party gains seats; for midterm election years a good year is when the incumbent party does not lose more than 23 seats. The predictions in column 2 are from the table equation, rounded to the nearest whole seat. On the basis of column 3, the average absolute prediction error = 7.91.

Forecasting House Seat Change

To begin an examination of the predictive abilities of the model (equation 4.3), look at the R-squared. By this standard, it performs very well. Some 90 percent of the variation in seat change is accounted for by the five variables. However, the R-squared by itself is an inadequate measure of forecasting quality, since it is a relative rather than an absolute measure. For a better idea of exactly how many seats off the predictions are likely to be, we need to examine the APE or the SEE.

The APE is 7.91 seats (see Table 4.4). This means that across these twenty-two elections, the model's predictions were off by an average of only about 8 seats per contest. Along with this low average error, an election-by-election examination (column 3, Table 4.4) suggests the errors are random in nature, not systematic. For example, the average midterm year prediction error of 7.5 seats is very similar to the average presidential year error of 8.4 seats. Likewise, the prediction error under Democratic presidents is 8.6 seats, compared with 7.5 seats under Republican presidents. There does not appear to be any temporal bias in the model either; the average error for the first half of the series (1948-1968) is 8.2 seats, and the average for the second half (1970-1990) is 7.6 seats. Hence, besides predicting House outcomes well in general, the model also manages consistent accuracy regardless of election type, party of the incumbent, or time period.

Although this accuracy is good, in terms of exact number of seats, it is certainly not perfect. Is the remaining error low enough that meaningful shifts in the political power composition of the House can be predicted? More particularly, can landslides and debacles be detected? Let us define a landslide or a debacle as contests with a net change of more than 30 seats for the president's party. Then there are two landslides—1948 (+75) and 1964 (+37)—and four debacles—1958 (−47), 1966 (−48), 1974 (−48), and 1980 (−33). Does the model predict these big swings accurately? Yes. In each case, a landslide (a gain of more than 30 seats) or a debacle (a loss of more than 30 seats) was correctly predicted.

While the model may be able to pick up gross shifts, such as landslides and debacles, it may miss the subtle shifts. Specifically, can it accurately sort out good years from bad years? Any definition of these terms must be adjusted for the big differences between midterm and presidential years. In the eleven presidential years of our series, the incumbent party gained seats five times and lost six times. Thus, for presidential election years, good is simply defined as no incumbent seat losses (while bad means seat losses). By way of contrast, in the eleven midterm years of our series the incumbent party always lost seats, for an average of −23.9. Therefore, for midterms, a good year is defined as below average (23 or fewer) losses, while a bad year means there were above average losses (24 or more seats). Applying these criteria to our model's predictions, we see that sixteen of the twenty-one elections are called correctly (columns 4 and 5 of Table 4.5). In terms of the outcome error measure devised in Chapter 3, this yields OE = .24. That is not that far from zero.

The model, then, is regularly able to predict actual seat shares with some precision. Further, this degree of precision allows the prediction of swings in the partisan composition of the House, both large and small. Thus, it can effectively track the changing balance of power in that body.

Table 4.5 Stability of the House Model

(1) Sample of elections	(2) Sample size (N)	(3) R^2	(4) SEE
1948-1990	22	.90	10.30
1948-1988	21	.91	10.40
1948-1986	20	.91	10.41
1948-1984	19	.92	10.43
1948-1982	18	.92	10.71
1948-1980	17	.93	10.29
1948-1978	16	.93	10.19
1948-1976	15	.94	10.27
1948-1974	14	.95	10.10
1948-1972	13	.94	10.80
1948-1970	12	.95	11.10
1948-1968	11	.94	12.16
Random	11	.90	10.17

Note: Column 1 lists the elections included in each sample. The latest election is dropped row by row.

Although the model appears to be a potent forecasting tool, it rests on a relatively small set of observations, from elections that have already occurred. As we did with the presidential model, it will be useful to test its stability under different sample conditions. Therefore, we estimated our House equation using various sets of elections. The results are exhibited in Table 4.5. The first row in the table presents the R-squared and SEE for our full set of elections, 1948 to 1990. The second row reports the same statistics when the 1990 case is omitted. The third row reflects the predictive power of our model after the 1990 and 1988 cases are dropped. In the subsequent rows we continue dropping cases, until the sample size is cut in half, with just eleven elections (1948-1968). Observe the stability in the statistics. The R-squared stays at .90 or above, and the SEE is steady, increasing a seat or two only after the sample size is halved. Across these different samples, the model remains strong. As a final test, we selected eleven elections at random and fit the model to them. The summary statistics for this random sample show no evidence of decay.

Taken as a whole, the tests in Table 4.5 provide substantial evidence that our House equation is an accurate and reliable predictor of election outcomes. Regardless of the sample of elections examined, model performance continues at a high level. Once these relevant variables are taken into account, little prediction error remains.

Conclusion

House elections are, to an extent, a referendum on national issues and the performance of the president. A healthy economy and a popular chief executive spell decisive seat gains in the House. However, these positive effects may be blunted by contextual factors. The impact of the economic conditions varies considerably between presidential and midterm years. Potential seat gains can be largely offset when the incumbent party has many seats exposed. Beyond these circumstances, there exists a general trend for the incumbent party to do worse in the House the longer it controls the Oval Office. When we combine these factors in a regression equation the coefficients are informative, the summary statistics encouraging. Most important for our purposes, the model produces accurate predictions of House seat change. Moreover, stability tests suggest that the model is likely to generate respectable predictions in the future (such as 1992; see Chapter 9).

Notes

1. We observe that presidential popularity, for reasons discussed in Chapter 2, predicts incumbent support best when it is measured in the summer prior to the election. This timing has theoretical interest, not to mention its encouraging implications for forecasting. However, for measuring summer popularity, the choice of month is somewhat arbitrary. Other things being equal, we favor a month that is earlier rather than later, to increase lead time, a critical component of a good forecasting model. With the congressional model, we manage an extra month's lead by using June approval ratings, rather than July ones. The cost of this extra lead is small, since June and July approval ratings (1948-1988) are almost perfectly correlated, $r = .96$.
2. Two variables in the final presidential model seem absent from this congressional model—party identification and candidate appeal. It turns out, however, that they are captured to a great degree by the variables actually included in the model. First, candidate appeal: To some extent, of course, candidate appeal cancels out in the aggregation of the conflicting attributes of the many individuals who are running for the 435 seats. However, as Gary Jacobson (1987, chap. 6) makes clear, even in the aggregate there appear to be some systematic election-to-election differences in candidate quality. The incumbent party tends to run better candidates in years in which the economy is doing well and the president is more popular. Fortunately, both these variables—the economy and popularity—are directly included in our model.

   The inclusion of party identification in the model is less obvious. Note that we calculate the dependent variable as the change in incumbent party seats; that is, incumbent party seats held after the election (seats at time t), minus the number of seats the party held going into the election (seats at time t − 1). Erikson (1990) suggests that a better way to formulate the dependent variable would be simply to use the number of seats the incumbent party holds after election time (seats at time t). That is, move seats at time t − 1 (a "voting history" measure in his words) to the right-hand side of the equation, as an independent variable. As a test, we modified our model to use seats at time t as a dependent variable and seats at t − 1 as a predictor variable. The results showed that the coefficients and summary statistics were almost identical to those in our equation 4.3. The reason for this is that the slope for the "voting history" variable (seats at time t − 1) is very nearly 1.0 (precisely, .98). This makes it effectively equivalent to putting "voting history" on the left-hand side of the equation, which is exactly what we do in equation 4.3. We prefer our formulation because it is straightforward and because the SEE for our equation 4.3 was slightly lower than that for the Erikson formulation.

As this discussion shows, voting history is imbedded in the dependent variable in our model. Thus the inertia of party loyalty, or party identification, is taken into account. By putting seats at time t − 1 in our dependent variable, we are in effect controlling for voting history and focusing on other reasons why the partisan balance changes. At the individual level, the analogue might be a model with a dependent variable focusing on "switchers," people who vote for different parties from one election to the next.

3. Here are the model estimates when GNP (growth rate from the fourth quarter of the year prior to the election to the second quarter before the election) is substituted for the income variable. As one sees, there is some erosion of the t-ratios. However, overall model performance appears almost as good as that of equation 4.3.

$$\underset{}{HC} = \underset{(-1.51)}{-24.94} + \underset{(.86)}{1.37E} + \underset{(1.29)}{3.54(E \times M)} + \underset{(3.03)}{.72PP} - \underset{(-5.49)}{.95X} - \underset{(-2.44)}{7.96T}$$

$R^2 = .83$ Adj. $R^2 = .78$ $N = 22$
SEE = 13.57 D-W = 2.18

CHAPTER 5

Senate Elections

The Constitution requires that legislation pass both chambers of Congress before becoming law. Thus support in the House is not enough to enact a president's programs; Senate approval is also necessary. Many a chief executive, with important legislation stalled in one chamber or the other, has cursed the bicameral structure of Congress. And while our Founding Fathers might have sympathized, they could contend that such frustration is a small price to pay for a legislative branch that incorporates the principles of separation of powers and checks and balances. Indeed, the Framers might have viewed presidential consternation as evidence that Congress is functioning as intended—as a brake on White House desires.

Although both bodies have the ability to veto presidential initiatives, the Senate, in part because of its special powers with regard to treaties and appointments, has earned a reputation for standing up to the White House. The two hundred-year history of Senate-White House relations contains numerous instances of presidents' programs dying in the upper chamber. For example, in the late 1950s and early 1960s Presidents Eisenhower and Kennedy saw many of their civil rights proposals derailed by powerful southern senators. The chamber's willingness to flex its veto muscle suggests that, if we wish to understand the determinants of public policy, forecasting Senate election outcomes is at least as important as forecasting House elections.

From a scientific perspective, the study of Senate election outcomes lags behind that of House outcomes. This relative lack of scholarship once led some researchers to call the Senate the "forgotten side" of Congress (Hibbing and Alford 1982). In part the neglect, at least as far as predictive models are concerned, is practical. Senate elections have long been considered very difficult to foretell. As two seasoned observers of the assembly declared: Senate forecasters "don't put money on their predictions—and for good reason. They know how unpredictable [the Senate] is" (Mann and Ornstein 1984, 43).

The contention that Senate elections are unpredictable stems in part from the characteristics of the office. Senators serve for six years, and thus are supposedly more insulated from immediate political pressures than House members. Senate campaigns attract more money than House races because senators have larger constituencies. And, with only one-third of the 100 Senate seats up for election every two years—compared with all 435 House seats—the media can pay closer attention to Senate races. Taken together, these factors help create a lively campaign, generally with better challengers, and elections are thought to be more than simply referenda on the president. That is, Senate candidates are considered familiar enough to the electorate to be judged independently of the incumbent administration.

If prediction is possible, it may have to come from knowledge of each individual campaign. The serious forecaster might have to be familiar with the mood of voters in the each state, the issues (both local and national) in every campaign, and the personalities of all the candidates. After all, early scholarly efforts to avoid this costly, individual, campaign-by-campaign prediction strategy met with only limited success. The first nationwide, aggregate-level model applied to prediction of the party composition of the Senate managed an R-squared of only .33, suggesting that two-thirds of the variation in partisan seat change was beyond explanation (Hibbing and Alford 1982). Their finding reinforces the notion that, indeed, Senate elections are unpredictable.

In this chapter, we continue our work on the construction of a macro-level explanatory model to forecast Senate contests. We begin by reviewing the measurement of partisan change in the Senate, comparing it with change in the House in order to get a sense of the task. Next we borrow liberally from our House forecasting model, trying to generalize across chambers about the determinants of legislative election outcomes. Then, we offer a model for Senate election outcomes that follows the global features of our House model, at the same time accommodating measures for unique Senate characteristics.

Measuring Partisan Change: The Senate Compared with the House

A popular scholarly contention holds that patterns of partisan change differ from the Senate to the House. Thomas E. Mann and

Norman J. Ornstein state the case clearly when they write: "In the United States Senate, we rarely see substantial party shifts from one election to another. Even when the House shifts by party margins of 40 seats, the Senate rarely changes by more than a few. When it does, the change is usually cataclysmic" (1984, 43).

Is their assertion correct? To help decide, let us formalize the arguments the statement contains. The first postulate is that from one election to another, partisan seat change is smaller in the Senate than in the House. We can express this as a hypothesis (H):

> H_1: Average partisan House seat change exceeds average partisan Senate seat change.

The second postulate states that when seat change does occur in the Senate, it is more substantial, even "cataclysmic" in size. Thus,

> H_2: The largest partisan seat changes in the Senate exceed the largest partisan seat changes in the House.

Both hypotheses can be tested using our post-World War II data. Taking H_1 first, a crude test simply compares the average partisan seat change for the House and the Senate. The figure for the House is 22.3 seats (from averaging the absolute value of the net incumbent party House seat change in Table 4.2). For the Senate, the figure is 3.6 seats (from averaging the absolute value of the net incumbent party Senate seat change in Table 5.1). Evaluating the two averages, we see that the House value is substantially larger, thus implying that H_1 is confirmed by this test.

Our conclusion, however, must be considered tentative. If we restrict our analysis to raw seats, the House is bound to register a larger average change merely because it draws from 435 seats, whereas the Senate has only 100 seats (with just one-third contested in any given election). Thus, for meaningful comparison, we need to somehow correct for these size differences. One way is to adjust the partisan change scores, treating them as if they occurred in legislative bodies of the same size. That is, simply multiply the Senate score by 4.35, the number of times larger the House is than the Senate. Doing so, the new corrected Senate value is 15.7 seats (that is, 4.35×3.6). However, this adjustment does not really go far enough, for only one-third of the Senate seats (not all 100) are actually up. Therefore, an additional multiple of 3.00 ought perhaps to be applied, yielding a fully adjusted Seat seat shift of 47 (that is, 15.7×3). By this measure, H_1 is disconfirmed, for the Senate appears to have much more partisan change, at least relatively speaking, than the House.

What about H_2? Are the Senate's partisan seat changes more often cataclysmic than those of the House? Look at the most dramatic change in each chamber. Across our time series, the largest shift of seats in the

Table 5.1 Seat Change in the Senate and House

Election (incumbent party)	Partisan composition of Senate		Net seat gain or loss	
	Democratic	Republican	Senate	House[a]
1946 (D)	45	51	—	—
1948 (D)	54	42	9	75
1950 (D)	49	47	−5	−29
1952 (D)	47	48	−2	−23
1954 (R)	48	47	−1	−18
1956 (R)	49	47	0	−3
1958 (R)	64	34	−13	−47
1960 (R)	65	35	1	21
1962 (D)	67	33	2	−5
1964 (D)	68	32	1	37
1966 (D)	64	36	−4	−48
1968 (D)	57	43	−7	−4
1970 (R)	54	44	1	−12
1972 (R)	56	42	−2	12
1974 (R)	60	37	−5	−48
1976 (R)	61	38	1	−1
1978 (D)	58	41	−3	−16
1980 (D)	46	53	−12	−33
1982 (R)	46	54	1	−27
1984 (R)	47	53	−1	17
1986 (R)	55	45	−8	−5
1988 (R)	55	45	0	−2
1990 (R)	56	44	−1	−8

Notes: R = Republican, D = Democratic. The average absolute change = 3.6 for the Senate, 22.3 for the House.

[a]From Table 4.2.

House was 75 (in 1948) and the largest change in the Senate was 13 (in 1958). Fully correcting the Senate figure for size yields a value of 170 (that is, 13 × 4.35 × 3). Comparing these extreme scores, the most cataclysmic change has occurred, in a relative sense, in the Senate rather than the House.

For a more comprehensive review of seat swings in the two chambers, we can examine their standard deviations. This statistic summarizes the variation in a measure across all cases.[1] It gives us a good idea of how spread out scores are around some central value. The standard deviation for House seat change is 28.9, compared with a raw Senate score of only 4.87. However, once this Senate score is fully adjusted for size differences, it balloons to 64 (that is, 4.87 × 4.35 × 3). This suggests that from election to election, there is relatively much more change in the Senate.

On the basis of these results, we cannot reject H_2. The Senate, after all, does appear to have more explosive partisan swings than the House.

In sum, the Senate is more subject to partisan change than the House, in terms of the average and the spread of seat swings, once the relevant size differences are fully adjusted. Recognition of this greater relative variation may reinforce the idea that Senate election outcomes are difficult to predict. Nevertheless, the pattern of variation itself suggests that much the same forces are at work as with House elections. In fact, when we correlate seat change in the two assemblies, $r = .70$. While the link is far from perfect, it is strong nonetheless. If seat change can be successfully forecast in the House, there is reason to believe that it can be successfully forecast in the Senate.

The House Model Applied to the Senate

Our notion is that the macro-determinants of Senate election outcomes are essentially the same as House ones, at least after slight adjustments for cyclical and contextual differences. That is, in the aggregate, Senate voters appear to react to economic and noneconomic issues, punishing or rewarding the president's party. Again, apart from issues, partisan success depends on how many seats are exposed. Also, the electoral calendar sets the context, providing a temporal rhythm to the effects of other variables.

Ideally, we would estimate a Senate model that was identical, in form and substance, to the model already estimated for the House. Recall the independent variables: income, popularity, midterm election, exposure, and time in office (see equation 4.3). Conceptually, these variables pose no problem when transferred to a Senate model. However, largely because of the staggered two-year election system of six-year terms, certain of the measures must be slightly modified. In particular, exposure and time in office deserve adjustments. After considering those, we will move on to model estimation.

First, think about the meaning of the exposure measure, as applied to the Senate. In any given election, two-thirds of its 100 seats are not being contested. Nevertheless, suppose these two-thirds are included in arriving at the average long-run base number of party strength and seats exposed. (Recall the formula in Table 4.4.) The measure no longer correlates strongly with the dependent variable of seat change ($r = -.31$). Because not all seats are in the race, as in the House, a preferred exposure measure for the Senate becomes simply the number of seats the incumbent party actually has up for reelection. We call this measure short-term exposure (labeled X') to distinguish it from the long-term exposure measure (labeled X) more appropriate for the House.

Across our post-World War II data series, there has been a good deal of fluctuation in the short-term exposure the president's party has faced in the Senate. The range has been from a peak of 25 seats in 1964 to a low of 8 in 1970. When the number of incumbent seats exposed is great, losses tend to be high. To take a relatively recent example, in 1980 the incumbent Democrats under President Carter had 24 Senate seats on the line. Given such a considerable exposure, their large loss of 12 seats becomes more understandable. Moreover, the Carter example reflects a broader pattern, for the correlation between short-term exposure and Senate seat change is strong, $r = -.57$. For the Senate, as for the House, the quantity of vulnerable seats appears to be a decisive determinant of incumbent party fortune.

The next measurement issue has to do with incorporation of long-run effects, as captured in the trend variable time in the White House (T). When this variable, as measured for the House, is correlated with Senate seat change, the relationship is almost zero ($r = -.04$). Thus, for the Senate, long-term costs of governing do not appear detectable by this measure. This null result may come partly from the staggered election rhythms of the Senate. Some have argued, for example, that there is a periodic strong reaction against the president's party, what has been called a "six-year itch" to "throw the rascals" out.

How might this six-year itch hypothesis work? Take, for illustration, the 1980 and 1986 Senate elections. In 1980, the Republicans startled most political observers by making a net gain of 12 seats. Republican exuberance faded into worry, however, as the 1986 elections approached. In that year the 12 first-term GOP senators elected in 1980 faced the voters again. Not surprisingly, the Democrats recaptured many of these seats. Is there a regular six-year cycle of Senate election results? When we develop a variable especially for the Senate—incumbent seat change from six years before (labeled L)—we find it supports the hypothesis in a moderate way, correlating at $-.31$ with current seat change. This six-year lagged variable, L, rather than a counter variable for time in the White House, T, appears to hold more promise for modeling trend effects in the context of the Senate.

Based on the foregoing considerations, we propose a Senate seat change model with measures like the House one, except for the inclusion of the appropriately modified exposure and trend measures, X′ and L. In words, we might write,

$$\begin{matrix}\text{Senate}\\ \text{seat}\\ \text{change}\end{matrix} = \begin{matrix}\text{Income}\\ \text{growth}\end{matrix} + \begin{matrix}\text{Presidential}\\ \text{popularity}\end{matrix} + \begin{matrix}\text{Seats}\\ \text{exposed}\end{matrix} + \begin{matrix}\text{Six-year}\\ \text{cycle}\end{matrix} \quad \text{(Eq. 5.1)}$$

Here are the regression estimates for such a model, from the 1948-1990 data:

$$SC = 2.13 + 0.41E + 1.36{*}(E \times M) + 0.09{*}PP - 0.65{*}X' - 0.06L$$
$$\quad\;\; (0.59) \;\; (1.20) \quad (3.23) \qquad\qquad (1.95) \quad (-4.10) \;\; (-0.50)$$

$R^2 = .77$ Adj. $R^2 = .70$ $N = 22$
SEE = 2.64   D-W = 1.57

where SC = number of Senate seats gained or lost by the president's party; E = real disposable income six months before (measured as in equation 4.3 for the House); M = a midterm variable, with 0 = midterm, 1 = presidential election year; PP = presidential popularity in the June Gallup Poll; X′ = seats exposed in the short term (the number of seats the president's party has up for reelection); L = six-year Senate seat lag (the number of Senate seats the president's party won or lost six years before the current election); * = statistically significant at .05, one-tail, $|t| > 1.75$; the statistics are defined as with equation 4.3 for the House.

These results are encouraging in several ways. First, the same basic forces that operate on House seat change seem to be largely responsible for seat change in the Senate. Economic and noneconomic issues significantly determine how the president's party will do. When the economy is failing, the incumbent party loses seats, at least in a presidential election year. Moreover, administration performance in other areas makes a difference as well. As the president's approval rating drops, so does the number of seats the president's party wins in the Senate. Further, exposure has a big effect.

On the whole, then, the model is pleasing. Contrary to what is commonly argued, the outcomes of Senate contests appear predictable. The parallel to the House results is not exact, however. Long-term, cyclical forces operate differently. We have seen that incumbency time in the White House (T) relates poorly to Senate seat change. (Also, it fails the .05 significance test if included in the model instead of L.) Equation 5.1 indicates that neither income (E) in midterm years nor the six-year seat lag variable (L) is close to conventional significance levels. Once the effect of the other variables, such as popularity and exposure, is taken into account, these two variables do not really add much to the explanation.

These insignificant results suggest that the model is not quite right and should be reestimated. But first consider again the specification of the model. With the rejection of time in office (T) and six-year seat lag (L) from the model, no trends at all are taken into account. Are there other trends that we have ignored and that we could measure? One is long-term party differences in the electorate. In the postwar period under study, the Democrats have almost always had more loyalists than the Republicans, both in the electorate and in Congress. An implication is that, in the aggregate, Democrats should be able to hold on to their seats a bit better. To put it another way, as the leading party, Democrats will tend to have fewer vulnerable seats. In the Senate case, they may run more candidates but be relatively less vulnerable because they have a bigger numerical base. (For example, 17 seats up out of a Democratic majority of 55 gives a smaller percentage of exposed seats than does 16 seats up out of a Republican minority of 45.)

One method of taking this long-run, historic Democratic advantage into account is simply to include a "party of the president" variable in the model. With such a dichotomous variable (scored 0 = Republican, 1 = Democrat), we would expect a positive coefficient, indicating that Democrats will hold on to more seats.[2]

Therefore, we respecify slightly the Senate equation. In words, we might write,

$$\begin{matrix}\text{Senate} \\ \text{seat} \\ \text{change}\end{matrix} = \begin{matrix}\text{Income growth} \\ \text{in presidential} \\ \text{election years}\end{matrix} + \begin{matrix}\text{Presidential} \\ \text{popularity}\end{matrix} + \begin{matrix}\text{Seats} \\ \text{exposed}\end{matrix} + \begin{matrix}\text{Party of} \\ \text{the president}\end{matrix} \qquad \text{(Eq. 5.2)}$$

The new regression results are as follows:

$$\begin{aligned} SC = \underset{(0.86)}{2.17} + \underset{(4.77)}{1.44}{*}(E \times M) + \underset{(3.39)}{0.13}{*}PP - \underset{(-6.81)}{0.84}{*}X' + \underset{(2.92)}{3.52}{*}D \end{aligned}$$

$R^2 = .83$ Adj. $R^2 = .79$ N = 22
SEE = 2.25 D-W = 1.56

where the variables and statistics are as with equation 5.1; * = statistically significant at .05 or more, one-tail ($|t| > 1.74$); and the additional variable is D = president's party (0 = Republican, 1 = Democrat).

This respecification improves the model. It is more parsimonious, having a smaller number of independent variables. Further, the coefficients, which all achieve high levels of statistical significance, tell a plausible tale. For every additional 1 percent growth in income, the incumbent party can expect to pick up 1 or 2 more seats, at least during presidential election years. With regard to presidential approval, a jump of 8 percentage points ought to net the ruling party another seat. (That is, 8 × .13 = 1.04.)

Now examine the new variable, president's party. Its coefficient of 3.52 indicates that when a Democrat is president, the incumbent party can expect to hold on to 3 or 4 more seats. The incumbent loss from seats exposed (indicated by .84X') is partially offset when that incumbent is a Democrat. Perhaps because of the party's narrower electoral base,

Republican seat gains are more fragile. (An alternative way to model this effect is actually to include an interaction variable, D times X′. But the simple additive dummy variable for party of the president, D, is more straightforward.)

Of course, this greater Republican risk does not mean that Democrats do not suffer from exposure. On the contrary, the exposure (X′) and presidential party (D) coefficients, taken together, suggest that for every 10 seats exposed under a Democrat incumbent, they can expect to lose 5. [That is, $(.84 \times 10) - (3.52 \times 1) = 4.88$.] Nevertheless, these losses from exposure, Democratic or Republican, are not foreordained. They can be overcome, perhaps to a large degree, by a healthy economy and a popular president. Obviously, before any final incumbent seat change predictions are made, the scores on all the relevant independent variables need to be taken into account. Since our primary goal is prediction, we turn to direct examination of the model's potential in that regard.

Forecasting Senate Seat Change

Table 5.2 displays the Senate seat change predictions generated from equation 5.2. The year-by-year forecasts are extremely precise, and serve to corroborate the model's robust summary statistics ($R^2 = .83$, SEE = 2.25). Particularly notable are the five elections with no prediction error (see column 3), including three of the last six. This accuracy is reflected in an APE of only 1.68 seats. Overall, then, the model missed the actual seat change by less than 2 seats per contest, on average.

A careful examination of the prediction errors (column 3) suggests no underlying abnormal patterns. Average error for midterm years is 1.9 seats, comparable to the 1.5 for presidential years. Under Democratic and Republican presidents, the error is about the same (1.6 and 1.8, respectively). For the first part of the time series (1948-1968) the error is 2.0; it is close to the 1.4 for the later period (1970-1990). Last, the errors for debacles and landslides are well predicted. Across the four elections with the largest seat swings—one landslide (1948, +9) and three debacles (1958, −13; 1980, −12; and 1986, −8)—the average error is only 1.8 seats.

The model can be counted on, then, to track the big partisan seat swings in the Senate. How well does it track the smaller, more common swings, from a "good" to a "bad" year? As we did for the House model, we offer a simple prognostication rule to distinguish good from bad performances. For consistency, we use the same rule. In years of presidential election, a good year is when the incumbent party gains seats. In midterms, a good year is when the incumbent party does better than the long-run midterm average. Thus, a good midterm year is when the incumbent party does not lose more than 3 seats. When these rules

Table 5.2 Forecasting Accuracy of the Senate Model

SC = 2.17 + 1.44(E × M) + 0.13PP − 0.84X′ + 3.52D

Year (president's party)	(1) Actual seat change	(2) Predicted seat change	(3) Error (1) − (2)	(4) Forecast good or bad year?	(5) Forecast right or wrong?
1948 (D)	9	7	2	good	right
1950 (D)	−5	−7	2	bad	right
1952 (D)	−2	0	−2	bad	right
1954 (R)	−1	0	−1	good	right
1956 (R)	0	0	0	bad	right
1958 (R)	−13	−8	−5	bad	right
1960 (R)	1	4	−3	good	right
1962 (D)	2	−1	3	good	right
1964 (D)	1	2	−1	good	right
1966 (D)	−4	−4	0	bad	right
1968 (D)	−7	−4	−3	bad	right
1970 (R)	1	3	−2	good	right
1972 (R)	−2	−4	2	bad	right
1974 (R)	−5	−7	2	bad	right
1976 (R)	1	2	−1	good	right
1978 (D)	−3	−2	−1	good	right
1980 (D)	−12	−12	0	bad	right
1982 (R)	1	−2	3	good	right
1984 (R)	−1	−3	2	bad	right
1986 (R)	−8	−8	0	bad	right
1988 (R)	0	0	0	bad	right
1990 (R)	−1	−3	2	good	right

Notes: For presidential election years a good year is when the incumbent party gains seats; for midterm election years a good year is when the incumbent party does not lose more than 3 seats. For the president's party, D = Democratic, R = Republican. The predictions in column 2 are from the table equation, rounded to the nearest whole seat. On the basis of column 3, the average absolute prediction error = 1.68.

are applied, the model makes no mistakes (see Table 5.2). All twenty-two elections are properly predicted in terms of whether they were good or bad for the incumbent party, yielding an OE = .00.

By these various tests, the Senate equation seems to perform well. But how stable is it? As with our previous models, we examine how it holds up when estimated on different samples. In Table 5.3, we drop elections one by one from the full sample, arriving at a sample size of half the original. The R-squared is strong and consistent across all sets of elections, ranging from .82 to .92. The SEE also stays low throughout the series, never rising above 2.7. We conclude that the Senate model, like the presidential and House models, is well grounded empirically.

Table 5.3 Stability of the Senate Model

Sample of elections	Sample size (N)	R^2	SEE
1948-1990	22	.83	2.25
1948-1988	21	.84	2.27
1948-1986	20	.84	2.34
1948-1984	19	.82	2.42
1948-1982	18	.84	2.43
1948-1980	17	.86	2.37
1948-1978	16	.82	2.47
1948-1976	15	.82	2.57
1948-1974	14	.82	2.70
1948-1972	13	.85	2.57
1948-1970	12	.91	2.23
1948-1968	11	.92	2.28
Random	11	.85	2.22

Note: Column 1 lists the elections included in each sample. The latest election is dropped row by row.

Comparing the House and Senate Models

Earlier, we speculated that House and Senate election outcomes are influenced by essentially the same forces. Now that we have developed both House and Senate forecasting models, a more direct test of this hypothesis is possible. Let us begin our comparison by reviewing the variables used in the models. Certain ones are identical. Both House equation 4.3 and Senate equation 5.2 include presidential popularity (PP), income growth (E), and election type (M). One other important variable, exposure (X or X′), is measured in numbers of seats for both models. Finally, each model contains a variable that taps long-term trends (either T or D). Thus, the basic structure of the two models is similar. Moreover, the variables all have statistically significant coefficients. Finally, both models perform well in terms of the summary statistics (that is, the R-squared are high and the SEE are low).

Given that election outcomes in the Senate and the House appear similarly determined, a logical next step is to compare the relative influence of the determinants. In particular, compare the specific magnitudes of the regression coefficients in House equation 4.3 and Senate equation 5.2. However, a direct comparison can be tricky, because of measurement and variance differences. One remedy is to "standardize" the scores of each variable in terms of its own variation (measured by its standard deviation) before running the regression.[3] This yields slope

Table 5.4 Comparison of Regression Coefficients (Standardized) for the House and Senate Models

Variable	House	Senate	Rank
Income by election type (E × M)	.44	.50	(2,2)
Income (E)	.13	.00	(4,4)
Popularity (PP)	.25	.38	(3,3)
Exposure (X or X′)	−.58	−.79	(1,1)

Notes: The variables from equation 4.3 are standardized for the House. The variables from equation 5.2 are standardized for the Senate. The last column gives the rank order of the magnitude of that variable's coefficient for the House and Senate, respectively.

coefficients that indicate the standard deviation change in the dependent variable, per one standard deviation change in the particular independent variable. Given that the variables are measured in a meaningful way, as these are, comparison of these standardized coefficients can tell us something about the relative impact of equivalent shifts in the independent variables. In Table 5.4 are presented the standardized coefficients for the variables in both models (except for the long-term trend variables, T and D, which are different enough that such comparison would make little sense).

The standardized coefficients suggest that, at least roughly speaking, these variables exercise a comparable impact irrespective of the chamber. The clearest example comes from the variable of income during presidential election years, with a House coefficient of .44 and a Senate coefficient of .50. The coefficients imply that a change in income of one standard deviation would shift seat change about half a standard deviation, in either the House or the Senate. The other coefficients do not compare as closely. Nevertheless, the rank order of the magnitude of effects is preserved: exposure always has the biggest effect, followed by income during presidential election years, and then presidential popularity. A last test of comparability remains. Do the two congressional models account for seat change equally well? An examination of the R-squared suggests that the answer is yes. Both the House and the Senate equations fit the data to about the same degree, with $R^2 = .90$ and .83, respectively.

Regardless of how we compare the House and Senate forecasting models, we find strong parallels. The independent variables are similar, the standardized coefficients are similar, and the overall fit of the models is similar. House and Senate elections are anything but unrelated events. By understanding the determinants of election outcomes in one chamber, we can know a great deal about the determinants of election outcomes in the other.

Conclusion

Conventional wisdom has held that Senate elections defy prediction. The unique characteristics of this body, it was argued, made forecasting a very chancy enterprise. As we have discovered, relatively speaking Senate results are highly variable. However, relying on theoretical guidance from aggregate prediction efforts for the House, a plausible model of Senate election outcomes can be developed. In fact, the model yields seat change predictions as precise as those of the House model offered in Chapter 4. Besides its accuracy, the common causal structure of the two models across chambers is noteworthy. Further, the models share a theoretical core with the presidential forecasting model, in terms of the role of economic and noneconomic issues. Nevertheless, attractive as these models may be, they are not the only ones available. Other scholars have proposed other explanations for the same phenomena. Perhaps these rival models are more compelling theoretically. And perhaps they are better at forecasting. In the next chapter, we evaluate these possibilities.

Notes

1. Often we want to know how spread out scores on a variable are. For instance, do the seat change scores bunch up around the average score, or are they widely scattered along a range of values? We have already gotten some sense of this from looking at the cataclysmic changes. A more general measure of the spread of these scores comes from calculation of the standard deviation statistic, whose formula is

$$\text{s.d. of X} = \sqrt{\frac{\Sigma(X_i - \overline{X})^2}{N}}$$

   where s.d. = standard deviation; X_i = observations on the variable X; $\overline{X}$ = average score on the variable X; N = number of observations.

   When this formula is applied to the Senate seat change variable, we see s.d. = 4.87. This confirms our informal observation that seat change in the Senate from election to election is not tightly clustered around the average score.
2. The reader may wonder whether a political party variable should, by this reasoning, also be included in the House model of Chapter 4. Actually, it already is. The long-term exposure measure (X) in the House model automatically adjusts for Democratic dominance in its calculation (by subtraction of the long-term average number of seats the party has held; see Table 4.4).

3. A variable X can be standardized by application of the following formula, which converts the raw scores on the variable into standard deviation units from the mean:

$$X_s = \frac{X_i - \overline{X}}{\text{s.d. of } X}$$

where X_s = standardized variable, X_i = observations on the variable X; $\overline{X}$ = average of the observations on X; s.d. of X = the standard deviation of the variable X (calculated from the formula in note 1).

CHAPTER 6

National Election Outcomes: Rival Models

Throughout the book, we focus on the prediction of aggregate-level, nationwide election outcomes. Of course, other election studies, several of which have already been cited, also look at the data from a national, systemic perspective. In this chapter, we compare our work with these rival models. One benefit of such an exercise is an increased appreciation of the varied explanations that can account for a given election result. Another benefit, the one most important for us, is the opportunity to evaluate these competing models as forecasting instruments.

We will consider the two most active objects of American national election research for which rival aggregate models exist in abundance—the president and the House of Representatives. (For the Senate, the only other models are Hibbing and Alford [1982] and Abramowitz and Segal [1986]; the latter yields results not unlike ours.) First, we describe in words the basic explanatory structure of each model. Then we illustrate the operation of the most current ones. Finally, we set down standards for judging their quality as forecasting tools and we compare them accordingly.

Presidential Election Models

Perhaps surprisingly, there are at least nine competing models of presidential election outcomes (see Table 6.1). They have a good deal in common. All but one are national, time series models. That is, the data are gathered on the nation as a whole, across a string of elections. (The lone exception is Rosenstone [1983], whose unit of study is the states.)

Table 6.1 Rival Presidential Election Outcome Models

Source	Explanatory variables
Abramowitz (1988)	Popularity (May), GNP (2d quarter), incumbency
Brody and Sigelman (1983)	Presidential popularity (last Gallup)
Campbell and Wink (1990)	Trial-heat question, GNP change (2d quarter)
Erikson (1989)	Hibbs's income, Tufte's "likes" measures
Fair (1978, 168)	GNP (2d and 3d quarter), time, incumbency
Hibbs (1982, 394)	Personal income (weighted over 15 quarters)
Lewis-Beck and Rice (Chapter 3)	GNP, popularity, House vote, primary margin
Rosenstone (1983, 74-75)	Welfare issues, income, incumbency, region, religion, war, congressional support
Tufte (1978, 122)	Income (election year), survey "likes"

Sources: It is impossible to capture fully the richness of each model in a tabular summary. Before reaching final conclusions, the reader should consult the original texts.

Typically, popular vote share in the post-World War II elections is predicted from a small set of explanatory variables. (Only Fair [1978, 1982, 1988] includes elections before 1948.) Almost always, economics looms large as a determinant. Still, there are important differences in the overall explanations offered. The table summarizes the key explanatory variables in models of leading analysts. (In selecting specific models from each author, we tried to represent the work fairly. To make a final judgment, the reader should consult that research directly.)

Of all the models, which offers the most promising explanation? Obviously, our theoretical commitment lies with the model we presented in Chapter 3. We believe it is a faithful representation of the individual vote choice writ large. However, the scholars represented in Table 6.1 might disagree. Happily, we do not have to resolve a debate about which explanation is better; we merely want to evaluate the models in terms of their performance as forecasting instruments. Before we begin, it is worth emphasizing that most of the models were designed primarily for explaining rather than forecasting. Although a better explanation tends to give a better prediction, that relationship is not perfect. Indeed, a particular model may offer a good theory but forecast poorly. Our evaluation sticks to forecasting properties. As an introduction, let us evaluate the forecasting properties of the two most recent presidential election outcome models, Erikson (1989) and Campbell and Wink (1990).

Erikson's (1989) effort is especially useful, combining the results of two theoretically and empirically powerful earlier models by Tufte (1978) and Hibbs (1982, 1987). From the former, he adopted the measure C, net candidate advantage, based on the University of Michigan's National Election Surveys' (NES) measures of what respondents "liked" and "disliked" about the candidates. From the latter, he took the measure I, income change over the last four years. Here are his regression results (Erikson 1989, 568):

$$V = 44.64 + \underset{(5.28)}{2.77I} + \underset{(4.31)}{6.50C} + e \qquad \text{(Eq. 6.1)}$$

SEE = 2.21 N = 10
Adj. R^2 = .888 D-W = 2.10

where V = percentage of the popular vote (for the two major parties) going to the candidate of the president's party; I = weighted average of yearly percentage change in disposable income per capita, cumulated over the fifteen quarters before the election quarter; C = net candidate advantage ("like" responses over "dislike" responses with regard to personal characteristics of candidates in NES election data); e = error; figures in parentheses are t-ratios; R-squared is adjusted to correct for the small sample size; N = number of observations (elections 1948-1984); D-W = Durbin-Watson test.

How does the Erikson model look, when evaluated only as a forecasting equation? Fortunately, he reports several of the different evaluation statistics we have come to use. Note that the R-squared, even adjusted, is very high, rounding to .89. Such an excellent fit implies that the model will generate a low prediction error. Examining the standard error of estimate itself, we see a fairly low 2.21. This suggests that out-of-sample, or future election, forecasts will be off by little more than 2 percent (in approximately two out of three calls). Regrettably, neither the absolute prediction error (APE) nor the win-lose error (OE) was offered.

Still, in terms of the R-squared and the SEE, the Erikson model appears to hold much promise. But for a forecaster it has a fatal flaw, one shared by two other models (those of Tufte and of Rosenstone) in Table 6.1. That is, it has *no* lead time. More precisely, the measure on net candidate advantage is not available until *after* the election, when the NES data are released. Thus, forecasting—predicting in advance of the election—is impossible. While the Erikson model may (and does) have considerable appeal in other ways, it simply is not usable in this respect.

The second current modeling effort under discussion here is that of Campbell and Wink (1990), which does have lead time. Their study is explicitly interested in forecasting, particularly from the Gallup trial-heat question: "If the presidential election were being held today, would you vote for the Republican candidate [*name*] or the Democratic candidate [*name*]?"

Developing an earlier idea in the literature (Lewis-Beck 1985), they combine trial-heat results, H, with second quarter GNP growth, G, to form a very potent model. Here are their strongest regression results (Campbell and Wink 1990, Table 2):

$$V = 24.34 + \underset{(10.6)}{.53H} + \underset{(5.8)}{2.14G} + e \qquad \text{(Eq. 6.2)}$$

SEE = 1.40 N = 11
Adj. R^2 = .95

where V = popular vote share, measured as in equation 6.1; H = percentage in favor of the presidential party's candidate in the trial-heat question posed by Gallup in late September; G = second quarter growth in real GNP per capita; statistics defined as with equation 6.1; N = number of observations (elections 1948-1988).

The Campbell/Wink model has several things to commend it in terms of forecasting. The R-squared is the highest of all the models under study. (The adjusted R-squared of our model in equation 3.5 is slightly lower, at .92.) Further, the SEE is low, lower than Erikson's, for example. Indeed, it compares favorably to the SEE from our model. (This comparison requires a conversion, since our SEE is measured in electoral votes. Recall from Chapter 3, note 1, that a 1 percent shift in popular vote yields a 4.27 percent shift in electoral vote; therefore, the SEE of Campbell/Wink converts to 4.27 × 1.40 = 5.98 percent of the electoral vote.) However, the low level of the SEE for the Campbell/Wink model, not to mention the Erikson model, is somewhat exaggerated since they both look only at the two-party vote share. On balance, though, in terms of these critical measures of R-squared and SEE, the Campbell/Wink model certainly appears to be a competitive performer.

From a forecasting perspective the principal weakness of the model, one that it shares with three other models (Brody and Sigelman, Fair, and Hibbs), is short lead time. The trial-heat data are gathered in late September and released even later. Thus the model can generate forecasts only about one month before an election. This lead time is so short that the forecast is of limited interest. The results of the actual contest are known very soon afterward.

In sum, two factors seem critical for a good forecasting model: accuracy and lead time. The need for accuracy is obvious. And unless all the indicators of a model are measured sufficiently in advance of the election date, forecasts become either impossible or trivial. In Table 6.2, the accuracy of each of the models is assessed by giving the SEE and the

Table 6.2 Forecasting Accuracy and Lead Time of Rival Presidential Models

Model	R^2	SEE	Lead time	Quality (Q)[a]
Abramowitz (1988)[b]	.90[c]	1.99%	long	.75
Brody and Sigelman (1983)	.71	4.02	short	.25
Campbell and Wink (1990)	.95[c]	1.40	short	.375
Erikson (1989)	.89[c]	2.21	none	.00
Fair (1978)	.70	4.02	short	.25
Hibbs (1982)	.63	5.09	short	.125
Lewis-Beck and Rice (Chapter 3)	.92[c]	2.13[d]	long	.75
Rosenstone (1983)	.93	4.5	none	.00
Tufte (1978)	.94	[e]	none	.00

Sources: It is difficult to choose one model when an author has published several. Our general selection principle was to select the first model appearing in print. Of course, certain authors have published revisions, subsequent to their original models. The careful forecaster will want to consult these efforts: Fair 1982, 1988; Hibbs 1987, 195-200; and Rosenstone 1985.

Notes: The following accuracy scores were assigned, based on the R-squared and the SEE: Abramowitz, 3; Brody and Sigelman, 2; Campbell and Wink, 3; Erikson, 3; Fair, 2; Hibbs, 1; Lewis-Beck and Rice, 3; Rosenstone, 2; Tufte, 3. The following lead time scores were assigned, distinguishing between no lead time (given a value 0), short lead (about a month in these cases, given a value 1), and long lead (in these cases about 4 months, given a value 2): Abramowitz, 2; Brody and Sigelman, 1; Campbell and Wink, 1; Erikson, 0; Fair, 1; Hibbs, 1; Lewis-Beck and Rice, 2; Rosenstone, 0; Tufte, 0.

[a]The quality score (Q) is based on the formula in the text.
[b]Figures based on the update to 1988 reported in Campbell and Wink (1990); this update makes comparison of this serious rival more straightforward.
[c]Adjusted R-squared.
[d]Popular vote error, estimated from electoral vote error for purposes of comparison.
[e]Not reported.

R-squared (usually unadjusted, since that is all the majority of authors report.) Also, the lead time of each is evaluated, as either none, short, or long. (Since several models were not designed with forecasting in mind, it is not surprising that they have little or no lead time.) We can see that two models have especially high levels of accuracy and lead—Abramowitz and Lewis-Beck/Rice.

In comparing the two, the adjusted R-squared and the SEE appear virtually identical when estimated on the same elections, 1948-1988. (The APE for the original Abramowitz [1988] model, at 1.2, is slightly higher than ours. For the Lewis-Beck/Rice model, recall that converted popular vote APE was .86.) Furthermore, the models are the only two with nontrivial lead time, both using indicators available by midsummer. Thus, in terms of accuracy and lead, they appear to be of comparable forecasting quality.

This quality measure can be formalized in the calculation of a simple formula,

$$Q = \frac{A \times l}{m}$$

(Eq. 6.3)

where Q = a measure of the forecasting quality of a model; A = a measure of accuracy; l = a measure of lead time; m = maximum score possible for the numerator (which is included merely to give Q a theoretical upper limit of 1.0).

In equation 6.3 we propose that the quality of a forecasting instrument is determined by two important factors, accuracy and lead time. Further, since lead time is a *necessary* condition, it is multiplied by accuracy. Put another way, if there is no lead time (l = 0), then a forecast is impossible, and the quality score of the model should be 0. Any accuracy multiplied by 0 will result in a 0 quality score. Now, to assign Q scores to the different models under study, we simply rank each on the accuracy variable as follows: perfect (4), high (3), medium (2), low (1), or none (0). Similarly, with regard to the lead time variable, we score each as none (0), short (1), or long (2). Take the Abramowitz model as an example. It has high accuracy (3) and long lead time (2), yielding a Q = .75, that is,

$$Q = \frac{3 \times 2}{8} = .75$$

In the last column of Table 6.2, the Q scores on the different presidential models are reported.

Many explanatory macro-models of presidential election have been developed. Evaluating them just in terms of forecasting criteria, we find that some are clearly preferred. It is risky to say which is the best. Nevertheless, over the long run, after several more elections are added to the series, a few should emerge as decidedly better at predicting the results. This shake out will help scholars determine which offers the better explanation of success in presidential contests.

House Election Models

With the study of House election outcomes, there are again many aggregate-level, time series models to compare. In Table 6.3 we try to give a fair summary of the explanations from nine leading models. All are

Table 6.3 Rival House Election Outcome Models

Source	Explanatory variables
Campbell (1986a)	Presidential vote, presidential popularity
Erikson (1990, 384, 391)	Past House vote
Hibbs (1982, 410)	Average of past income (1st to 6th quarter of presidential term)
Jacobson (1989, 786, Table 8)	Challenger quality, seats last election, challenger quality times presidential popularity
Kramer (1971, 140-141)	Election year per capita personal income
Lewis-Beck and Rice (Chapter 4)	Income, presidential popularity, risk, incumbent tenure
Marra and Ostrom (1989, 556)	Presidential popularity, change popularity, party identification, seats at risk, political events
Oppenheimer, Stimson, and Waterman (1986)	Seats exposed
Tufte (1978, 112)	Election year income, fall Gallup Poll

Note: A full appreciation of the models can be gotten only by consulting the original sources directly. Several authors have published more than one model: see, for example, Campbell 1985, 1986b, 1987; Jacobson and Kernell, 1983; Hibbs, 1987.

supported by regression equations estimated on post-World War II congressional elections (except for Kramer, who began with 1896). While the explanatory variables indicate considerable diversity from scholar to scholar, certain common themes bear mention. First, in terms of broad theory, the studies emphasize either a national or a local interpretation of the vote choice. A principal advocate for the latter would be Jacobson and Kernell (1983). Also speaking for this local perspective, Thomas Mann (1978, 1) contends that "in deciding how to cast their ballots, voters are primarily influenced not by the President, the national parties, or the state of the economy, but by the local candidates."

Among those who see congressional elections from a national perspective, a further useful distinction is between presidential coattails and referenda theories. The former, coming out of Angus Campbell's (1964, 1966) work on surge and decline, argues that congressional vote preference is largely determined by presidential preference. A popular presidential candidate pulls along many House candidates on his coattails, and coattails are inevitably shortened by the midterm. Currently, the work of James Campbell (1986, 1987) best represents the coattails tradition.

Tufte (1975, 106) nicely sums up the second, complementary, national perspective, when he claims that "overall election outcomes represent a referendum on the incumbent administration's handling of

Table 6.4 Evaluating Rival House Election Models

Source	Outcome predicted	Elections studied	Lead time
Campbell (1986a)	seats	midterms	short
Erikson (1990)	votes	midterms	long
Hibbs (1982)	votes	midterms	short
Jacobson (1989)	seats	all elections	none
Kramer (1971)	votes	all elections	none
Lewis-Beck and Rice (Chapter 4)	seats	all elections	long
Marra and Ostrom (1989)	seats	all elections	none
Oppenheimer, Stimson and Waterman (1986)	seats	all elections	long
Tufte (1978)	votes	midterms	none

Note: "Lead time" refers to how long in advance of the election the model can actually be used to generate a forecast ("none" means necessary data are not available until after the election; "short" means necessary data are available only a month or so before the election; "long" means necessary data available at least four months before).

the economy and of other issues." In other words, the voter judges how the president's party is managing the nation; if that judgment is favorable, the vote is for the congressional candidate of the president's party. Otherwise, it is against. Further, among the authors who test some version of this referenda theory, a key question is whether it operates across all elections (for example, see Kramer 1971) or across midterm elections only (see the discussion in Erikson 1990, 394-397).

Evidently, the competing models are theoretically very rich. They also offer different forecasting possibilities, as Table 6.4 indicates. Unfortunately, certain important differences among the models make comparison more difficult than in the presidential case. First, about half the studies examine midterm elections separately, whereas the rest combine all elections (midterm and presidential year) into one model. This shifting sample base makes the uncritical comparison of R-squared tricky. (Although it can be said that most of the model R-squared values are, encouragingly, at .8 or better.) Second, the studies are about evenly divided in terms of whether they predict the actual number of seats a party will win or merely the percentage of votes for a party. This measurement difference in party support turns comparison of the SEE into an apples-and-oranges problem.

However, useful comparisons can still be made. We can impose some order by laying down guidelines for a good House forecasting model. Suppose the goal is to reduce prediction error. Other things being equal, the larger the sample, the smaller the error. Therefore, we focus on models that include all elections, not just midterms. This effectively doubles the sample size (while permitting any midterm differences to be built into the model). Another source of error comes from the translation of votes into seats. This swing ratio, as it is called, is necessary in order to predict how many seats the party will actually win from their votes (Tufte 1974). Since the translation of votes into seats is never perfect, models that use votes as the predicted variable have this added source of forecasting error. Therefore, we prefer models that directly predict seats, not votes.

If we confine ourselves to models that both cover all elections and predict seats we isolate three, besides our own: Oppenheimer/Stimson/Waterman; Jacobson; and Marra/Ostrom. The Oppenheimer/Stimson/Waterman (1986, Table 1) model of incumbent seats exposed has great parsimony and conceptual appeal. However, the one predictor variable of seats exposed manages an R-squared of only .48, far from the statistical fits of the other two models. Further, of all the efforts in the literature, those of Jacobson (1989) and Marra and Ostrom (1989) are the most recent. Hence, it seems appropriate that we review them for their forecasting potential.

We begin with Jacobson because his perspective is the least like ours. Recall that, as a general theoretical orientation, Jacobson (1989, 774-775) sees congressional contests as local affairs: "The choice offered locally between candidates is thus the main focus of electoral politics. In contests between House incumbents and challengers, the nature of the choice is shaped largely by the political talents and campaign resources of the challenger." A key factor in the Jacobson explanation of the congressional voter, as this quotation makes clear, is candidate quality. The notion that more qualified candidates do better has been pursued by Jacobson (and Kernell) extensively and persuasively in various publications (see especially Jacobson and Kernell 1983, Jacobson 1987). By way of illustration, here is one of his early regression models (Jacobson 1981):

$$V = 42.8 + \underset{(2.45)}{.27Q} + \underset{(1.67)}{.78I} + e \qquad \text{(Eq. 6.4)}$$

Adj. $R^2 = .37$
$N = 9$

where V = national popular vote share for Republicans in House races; Q = difference in the percentage of each party's challengers who have held elected office; I = annual growth rate in real disposable per capita income, first quarter of the year before the election to the first quarter of the election year; N = the number of elections (presidential years only, 1948-1980); other statistics as in equation 6.1.

This model suggests that incumbent vote share is largely a function of economic performance (I) plus relative candidate quality (Q). When applied to 1984 the model gave a vote prediction of 47.4 percent for the Republicans, which, by application of a swing ratio, translated into an incumbent net seat gain of 17 (Lewis-Beck 1985, 59). In fact, the incumbent Republicans experienced a net gain of 14 seats, leaving only a +3 error. Although this point forecast is rather close, the overall model shows room for improvement. The R-squared is very low, only nine elections are included, and the dependent variable is votes, not seats.

In further efforts to explain congressional election outcomes, Jacobson has elaborated a fuller model. Here is an important recent modeling effort (Jacobson 1989, 784, Table 8, column 3):

$$S = 22.48^{**} + 6.51^{**}A - .42^{***}D + .52^{**}Q + .04(Q \times I) + .003^{*}(Q \times P) + e \quad \text{(Eq. 6.5)}$$

SEE = 2.8 (≅ 13 seats) N = 21
Adj. R^2 = .86 D-W = 2.09

where S = change from the last election in the percentage of seats won by the Democrats; A = party of the administration; D = percentage of seats won by the Democrats in the last election; Q = relative candidate quality, basically measured as in equation 6.4; (Q × I) = Q measure multiplied by change in real income per capita for the election year; (Q × P) = Q measure multiplied by presidential popularity as measured in the last Gallup Poll before the election; e = error; *, **, *** = statistically significant at .05, .01, and .001, one-tail, respectively; N = sample size, all congressional elections, 1946-1986; D-W = Durbin-Watson statistic; SEE = standard error of estimate (measured in percentage change, like the dependent variable; translated into seats, it equals about 13, working from Jacobson's note on the coefficient of .42, which "indicates a 1-percentage-point difference in relative challenger quality is worth almost two House seats" [Jacobson 1989, 785]).

The model suggests that Democratic party seat fortunes in the House can be largely predicted from at least three significant substantive factors: the number of seats exposed (D); the quality of their challengers relative to the Republicans (Q); and the relative quality of candidates in the context of a popular president (Q × P), which appears to indicate that politicians are strategic. The argument has theoretical appeal. Moreover, the accuracy statistics, R-squared and SEE, are as good as, or better than, most. However, perhaps because it was not formulated with forecasting in mind, the model runs afoul of the other important general standard: lead time. The presidential popularity data are from the last poll before the election, thus making for a short lead. The income data are from the entire election year itself (ending in December; see Jacobson

1989, 785). Thus, the Jacobson model poses a not uncommon dilemma for the congressional forecaster. A promising theoretical explanation may serve poorly, or not at all, as a forecasting equation.

This dilemma repeats itself in the work of Marra and Ostrom (1989, 553), who propose what they call a comprehensive referendum voting model, claiming it covers the elements of "(1) Tufte's Referendum Voting Model, (2) Fiorina's individual-level Retrospective Voting Model, and (3) Jacobson and Kernell's Strategic Politician Model." Substantively, it predicts incumbent seat change from current presidential popularity (X_1), personal income (X_2), political events (X_3), change in presidential popularity (X_4), party identification (X_5), and seats at risk (X_6). Here is their key regression equation (Marra and Ostrom 1989, 556):

$$S = -55.13* + 1.12*X_1 - 1.5X_2 + 1.45*X_3 + 1.16*X_4 + .22*X_5 - .31*X_6 + e \quad \text{(Eq. 6.6)}$$

$R^2 = .96$ Adj. $R^2 = .94$ APE = 4.09
SEE = 5.77 N = 19

where S = change in number of House seats for president's party; X_1 = presidential popularity in final Gallup Poll before election; X_2 = change in per capita real disposable income in third quarter of election year; X_3 = selected positive and negative political events; X_4 = "the difference between the highest level of Gallup Poll support in the *six months following the previous midterm or general election* and the most recent level of support prior to the midterm or on-year election"; X_5 = net percentage advantage in identification going to the party of the president, taken from the Michigan NES data except for 1950 and 1986; X_6 = number of House seats held by incumbent party compared to its average over the last eight elections; * = statistically significant at .05 or better; SEE = standard error of estimate of the seat change; N = number of elections, 1950-1986; APE = absolute prediction error within the sample.

The Marra/Ostrom explanation is interesting in many ways. At first blush, it holds great promise as a forecasting device. The R-squared is almost at 1.0. Further, the direct measures of prediction error, the SEE and the APE, are lower than those of any other model, including our own. However, as we have argued, accuracy is a necessary but not a sufficient condition for forecasting. Lead time is also needed. Lamentably, the Marra/Ostrom model includes predictors that are available only shortly before the election (that is, X_1 and X_3) or not available until after the election (that is, X_5). Thus, while the model may well fulfill its intention to provide a comprehensive *explanation* of House seat change, as a before-the-fact forecasting instrument it has limited utility.

Conclusion

Numerous explanatory models of national election outcomes have been proposed for both the president and the House of Representatives. These explanations are in some ways complimentary and in some ways opposed. All are tested against real election results, usually from the post-World War II period. The statistical tests help sort out which models are more promising, which less. In terms of their evaluation solely as forecasting tools, certain ones appear to provide a more optimal combination of the two principal criteria—accuracy and lead time. To forecasters, the final proof of the pudding comes in the quality of their ex ante predictions. Before elections, the models should be used to generate forecasts. With each passing election, evidence accumulates on these before-the-fact predictions. From this evidence, political scientists can begin to distinguish which models work, which do not. In this manner, the forecasting models are winnowed. Moreover, the explanatory models are winnowed as well, since good explanations tend to predict better than bad ones. Hence, the forecasting enterprise, while valuable in its own right, comes to serve the higher scientific purpose of explanation.

CHAPTER 7

Governors and State Legislatures

The Constitution provides for a federal form of government. Under this system, the national government in Washington shares power with state and local governments. Exactly how the power is to be shared has been hotly debated for the past two hundred years. In 1988, for instance, Washington and the states clashed over a national law that provided special highway funds to states that cracked down on drunk driving. Most state officials agreed with Washington that something needed to be done about drunk driving, but many opposed federal government intervention in this area. A spokesman for Governor Mike Sullivan of Wyoming summed up the states' position well when he said: "We don't like to be blackmailed by the Federal Government; we don't like to be dictated to . . . ; we don't like being told what to do" (*New York Times*, July 1, 1988, 7).

Despite the constant scuffles between different levels of government in the United States, the federal system has endured. The relative balance of authority between governments has fluctuated over time, but each level of government has always retained substantial power. In recent years there has been an effort to shift power away from the federal government and toward the states. Presidents Reagan and Bush have pushed for a New Federalism that curbs the size and influence of the national government in areas such as social welfare and categorical grants. (How difficult it is to change government administration and policies can be appreciated by reading Lewis-Beck and Squire [1990] on the New Era-New Deal transition.)

In the face of these efforts, state and local governments continue to exercise tremendous influence over our lives. States, for example, have always wielded extensive powers in the areas of taxation, spending, regulation, and justice. Almost every aspect of our daily routine is touched by state policies and procedures; for instance, states regulate our roadways, tax our purchases, establish health standards, stimulate the economy, and help fund education. Under American federalism, state and local governments obviously have power to make important policy.

These governments are constantly wrestling with the questions of how policies should be designed and implemented. For the most part, the battle is drawn along party lines. Every state holds partisan elections for governor, and every state except Nebraska elects a partisan state legislature. As in Washington, the parties in the states put forward different policy proposals; for instance, the Democrats tend to support a larger, liberal role for state government in the areas of assistance for the needy and regulation of the economy, and the Republicans tend to support a more limited, conservative role for government. (See the helpful current work on state policy by Erikson, Wright, and McIver 1989). Which view prevails depends in part on which party controls the governorship and the state legislature. As an example, Thomas Dye (1984) found that in many states welfare spending grew more quickly when Democrats were in power.

The critical role that partisan control of state government plays in determining state policy makes accurate forecasts of state elections valuable. Among other things, forecasts of the partisan makeup of the governorships and state legislatures would help us predict the future direction of state policy initiatives. But foretelling state election outcomes has ramifications outside state policy as well. For example, political pundits have long held that the party that controls the governorship has the upper hand in carrying that state in the next presidential election. As a political reporter put it, "Control of a statehouse is no guarantee that a political party will carry a state in a presidential election ... [but] politicians consider occupation of a Governor's office of major importance" (*U.S. News & World Report,* November 18, 1974, 29). State elections also have something to say about the partisan composition of Congress. Every ten years the state legislatures take the lead in redrawing congressional districts. The party that controls the legislature can set district boundaries in subtle ways to its advantage. National and state party organizations are well aware of this. In preparation for the redistricting that would take place after the 1990 elections, the parties spent millions of dollars in an effort to control as many state legislatures as possible (*Los Angeles Times,* February 21, 1989, 18).

In this chapter, we develop aggregate election outcome models to forecast the partisan makeup of governorships and the state legislatures. As a modeling guide, we borrow, at least initially, from theory that proved valuable in our presidential and congressional work.

Forecasting Gubernatorial Elections

Many political observers contend that gubernatorial election outcomes are determined by local concerns, not national issues like the economy and presidential performance. Prior to the 1969 gubernatorial elections, for example, *U.S. News & World Report* wrote that the election outcomes were "more likely to depend on local personalities and conditions" than on national affairs and that the results would not be "regarded as a referendum on the performance of the ... Republican Administration in Washington" (November 3, 1969, 27). After the Democrats won big in the gubernatorial contests of 1974, *Time* concluded, "Perhaps the most important reason for the Democrats' success was nothing more complicated than the fact that the party had generally managed to put forward the most attractive and distinctive candidates" (November 18, 1974, 16). Noted state politics scholar Malcolm Jewell (1968, 545-546) described such localist thinking when he wrote: "The governor is blamed for the lagging [state] economy, depressed areas, and spreading [state] unemployment."

Despite claims that gubernatorial election outcomes are the product of local issues, some political scientists have had difficulty substantiating this link empirically. For example, the innovative studies of John Chubb (1988), Patrick Kenney (1983), and Robert Stein (1990) find little, if any, association between state economic conditions and gubernatorial election results. If local conditions are not the primary determinant in these races, what motivates these voters? One suggestion from the aforementioned studies is that it is national issues. For example, Chubb (1988) and Samuel Peltzman (1987) show that a major factor influencing gubernatorial elections is the health of the national economy. In particular, Chubb (1988, Table 1) reports that presidential responsibility for change in national income growth has a highly significant effect on gubernatorial election outcomes. Given these findings, our national-level measures on economic growth and presidential approval may well help predict races for governor.

Before we formalize a model, we must clarify the meaning of partisan composition of American governorships over the 1946 to 1990 period. Table 7.1 presents these data (columns 1 and 2). The figures show that Democrats have generally held the majority of the governorships, averaging approximately 30 across the period. The variation has been substantial, however, with Democrats controlling as many as 37 seats in 1976 and as few as 18 in 1952. Republican strength reached a peak in 1968 with 31 governors and bottomed out at 12 in 1976.

Column 3 in Table 7.1 traces the presidential party's success in gubernatorial elections. On average, the party experiences a net loss of about 3 governorships every election year. In this way, at least, guberna-

Table 7.1 Partisan Composition of Governorships, 1946-1990

Year (president's party)	(1) Number of Democratic governors	(2) Number of Republican governors	(3) Net gain or loss for president's party
1946 (D)	23	25	—
1948 (D)	30	18	7
1950 (D)	23	25	−7
1952 (D)	18	30	−5
1954 (R)	27	21	−9
1956 (R)	28	20	−1
1958 (R)	35	14	−6
1960 (R)	34	16	2
1962 (D)	34	16	0
1964 (D)	33	17	−1
1966 (D)	25	25	−8
1968 (D)	19	31	−6
1970 (R)	29	21	−10
1972 (R)	31	19	−2
1974 (R)[a]	36	13	−6
1976 (R)[a]	37	12	−1
1978 (D)	32	18	−5
1980 (D)	27	23	−5
1982 (R)	35	15	−8
1984 (R)	34	16	1
1986 (R)	26	24	8
1988 (R)	28	22	−2
1990 (R)	29	21	−1
		Average change =	−2.95

Source: See Appendix.

Note: R = Republican, D = Democratic.

[a]Maine had an independent governor in 1974 and 1976.

torial elections resemble those for Congress: overall the incumbent party tends to lose seats. There is wide fluctuation, however. At the extremes, the party of the president lost 10 seats in 1970 and picked up 8 seats in 1986. How can this considerable variation in gubernatorial partisanship be explained? For an initial accounting, we borrowed the core measures of our congressional models: presidential popularity, economic growth, midterm status, and exposure. The first three variables are incorporated exactly as with the Senate model (equation 5.2). However, exposure has a slightly different meaning in this context, so it requires a slightly different measure.

Our exposure variable is calculated by subtracting the number of governorships the incumbent party is defending from the number of seats the other party is trying to protect. For example, in 1956 the incumbent party (Republican) controlled 15 of the 32 seats up for election and the out party (Democratic) held the other 17. Subtracting 15 from 17 yields 2, meaning that the in party had two fewer seats exposed than the out party. We rely on this relative exposure measure, rather than the simple raw number of incumbent seats up for reelection, because the number of gubernatorial races varies between midterm and presidential years. The importance of this becomes clear when we compare a year like 1968 with the 1956 example. In 1968 the incumbent party had 16 seats up for reelection, almost the same as in 1956, but the out party had only 8 seats to defend, less than half the 1956 number. Obviously, the opportunity for the incumbent party to pick up seats was smaller in 1968 than in 1956, while the chance of losing seats was essentially the same in both years.

Another contextual feature of gubernatorial races is the fact that a few states have held their elections in odd-numbered years, neither presidential nor midterm years. At present five states follow this practice. Virginia and New Jersey hold elections in November of the year following presidential elections; Mississippi and Kentucky hold elections in November of the year before presidential elections; and Louisiana holds its election in October of the year before presidential elections. (We assign these few elections to the next even year.)[1]

When these core variables of popularity (PP), the economy at midterm, and relative exposure (XR) are entered in a regression equation predicting incumbent party seat change, the results are as follows:

$$GC = -8.60^{*} + 1.24^{*}(E \times M) + 0.09^{**}PP + 0.28^{*}XR \quad \text{(Eq. 7.1)}$$

$$(-3.06) \qquad (2.83) \qquad\qquad (1.69) \qquad\qquad (3.44)$$

$R^2 = .58$ Adj. $R^2 = .51$ N = 22
SEE = 3.33 D-W = 1.69

where GC = number of governorships gained or lost by the president's party; E = income (percentage change in real disposable personal income from the fourth quarter of the year before the election to the second quarter of the election year); M = midterm (scored 1 if a presidential election year, 0 otherwise); (E × M) = an interaction term; PP = Gallup presidential approval rating in June; XR = number of president's party's seats up for reelection subtracted from the number of out-party seats up for reelection; *, ** = statistically significant at .05 or .10, respectively, one-tail, $|t| > 1.73$, or 1.33, respectively; all the other variables and statistics are defined as with equation 5.2.

These estimates yield mixed results. It is encouraging that all three independent variables reach some conventional level of statistical significance. Forces that shape congressional and presidential elections also influence gubernatorial outcomes. However, strong as that influence may be, it still leaves considerable variance unexplained. Because we want to forecast, it would be useful to develop a more theoretically complete model.

Recall that our Senate equation included a trend variable, D, to capture the long-time Democratic party dominance. Its inclusion certainly seems worth considering here. Another potential trend variable, unique to the gubernatorial context, taps changes in the number of gubernatorial elections per year. As late as 1940, twenty-four states elected governors every two years. In response to growing concern that two-year terms resulted in "eternal ... electioneering," states slowly began to adopt four-year terms (Sabato 1983, 98). By 1960, the number of states with two-year terms had dropped to fifteen. Thereafter, the pace quickened; from 1970 to 1975 seven states switched to four-year terms. Currently, only four states elect a governor every two years. With fewer elections being held, the incumbent (president's) party becomes less able to gain or lose a big number of governorships. To measure this change in an uncomplicated way, we created a "longer term" (GT) variable scored 0 for election years 1948 to 1972 and 1 for years 1974 to 1990.

When we more fully specify the model by adding the party of the president (D) and the longer term (GT) variables to the gubernatorial equation, it yields the following regression results:

$$GC = -15.27* + 1.10*(E \times M) + 0.16*PP + 0.41*XR + 4.89*D + 3.64*GT \quad \text{(Eq. 7.2)}$$

$$(-5.72) \quad (3.19) \quad (3.65) \quad (5.42) \quad (3.30) \quad (3.15)$$

$R^2 = .80$ Adj. $R^2 = .73$ N = 22
SEE = 2.47 D-W = 2.24

where D = party of the president, scored 1 for Democratic and 0 for Republican; GT = longer term, scored 0 for elections 1948-1972 and 1 for elections 1974-1990; * = statistically significant at .05, one-tail, $|t| > 1.75$; all other terms and statistics are defined as with equation 7.1.

The estimates of equation 7.2 support this theoretical reformulation. All the independent variables have highly significant coefficients. Moreover, these coefficients tell an interesting story about the forces that move gubernatorial elections. The economy/mid-term coefficient (for E $\times$ M) indicates that in presidential election years the incumbent party can expect to win an additional governorship for every 1 percent increase in income. Further, the incumbent party can anticipate picking

Table 7.2 Forecasting Accuracy of the Gubernatorial Model, 1948-1990

$$GC = -15.27 + 1.10(E \times M) + 0.16PP + 0.41XR + 4.89D + 3.64GT$$

Year (president's party)	(1) Actual seat change	(2) Predicted seat change	(3) Error (1) − (2)
1948 (D)	7	4	3
1950 (D)	−7	−5	−2
1952 (D)	−5	−5	0
1954 (R)	−9	−10	1
1956 (R)	−1	−1	0
1958 (R)	−6	−3	−3
1960 (R)	2	0	2
1962 (D)	0	−2	2
1964 (D)	−1	2	−3
1966 (D)	−8	−5	−3
1968 (D)	−6	−4	−2
1970 (R)	−10	−12	2
1972 (R)	−2	−2	0
1974 (R)	−6	−7	1
1976 (R)	−1	0	−1
1978 (D)	−5	−7	2
1980 (D)	−5	−7	2
1982 (R)	−8	−3	−5
1984 (R)	1	0	1
1986 (R)	8	7	1
1988 (R)	−2	−2	0
1990 (R)	−1	−1	0

Notes: Column 1 is the actual gubernatorial seat change for the incumbent party. Column 2 is the seat change predicted from equation 7.2. On the basis of column 3, average absolute prediction error = 1.64.

up an additional governorship for every 6-point increase in presidential popularity (that is, $.16 \times 6 = .96$). The exposure term (XR) says that the fewer seats the incumbent party has to defend compared with the out party, the better it will fare. For example, suppose the in party has 15 seats up, while the out party has 17. This gives an exposure score of 2, which means the incumbent party would expect a net gain of about one governorship (that is, $.41 \times 2 = .82$).

The two new variables added to the model, D and GT, also have persuasive interpretations. In particular, when the White House is under Democratic control, that party can anticipate approximately 5 more governorships. The superior institutional and electoral strength of the Democrats appears to yield the party extra benefits in the statehouses. The final variable, GT, taps the shift from two-year terms to four-year terms for governors. Its coefficient implies that the incumbent party has lost an average of 3 to 4 fewer seats per election since 1974. The move to four-year terms means fewer contests per election year and, necessarily, fewer opportunities for the incumbent party to lose seats.

Overall, this model appears to perform well, with an R-squared of .80 and an SEE of 2.47. But does the model predict individual elections accurately? Table 7.2 compares the actual incumbent seat changes over the 1948-1990 period with the predictions generated by our equation. The results show that, year by year, the predictions have little error. For example, in only five of the twenty-two elections does the predicted partisan change in governors miss the actual partisan change by more than 2 (see column 3). This precision is summarized in the low APE of 1.64.

In addition to this forecasting record, the model helps to further the contemporary finding of other scholars that gubernatorial elections are heavily influenced by national conditions. Macroeconomic fluctuations and presidential popularity, in particular, play an integral role in shaping the partisan character of governors' offices, much as they do for the Congress and the White House.

Forecasting State Legislative Elections

In many ways, state legislative races are the quintessential local political contests. The districts are relatively small, the candidates are often friends with many people in their districts. Door-to-door campaigning is very common. Local issues, such as improving schools and roads, may appear to dominate the agenda. The idea that somehow national affairs impinge on down-home contests might seem far-fetched. Recent research, however, suggests that state legislative races are influenced by how well the incumbent president runs in the state (Bibby 1983; Campbell 1986c). If the national economy is expanding and the president is handling other issues well, many people will reward the president's party by voting for the party's state legislative candidates. In other words, the same national-level hypotheses that predict presidential, congressional, and gubernatorial elections should also be important in forecasting state legislative outcomes.

Before turning to the data analysis, we need to decide on a measure of partisan change in the state assemblies. We could use individual legislators as our indicator, tallying up how many Democrats and Republicans serve in all the states. But this would be too disaggregated, ignoring the geographic context of the races. A more appropriate aggregate-level approach measures the state legislature as a whole, using the number of legislatures controlled by the president's party. By *controlled*

Table 7.3 Partisan Composition of State Legislatures, 1946-1990

Year (president's party)	(1) Both houses Democratic controlled	(2) Both houses Republican controlled	(3) Split partisan control	(4) Change in incumbent party control
1946 (D)	17	25	4	—
1948 (D)	19	15	12	2
1950 (D)	19	21	6	0
1952 (D)	16	26	4	−3
1954 (R)	19	20	7	−6
1956 (R)	22	18	6	−2
1958 (R)	31	7	10	−11
1960 (R)	27	15	6	8
1962 (D)	24	16	8	−3
1964 (D)	33	6	9	9
1966 (D)	24	15	9	−9
1968 (D)	20	19	9	−4
1970 (R)	22	17	9	−2
1972 (R)	27	16	6	−1
1974 (R)	37	4	8	−12
1976 (R)	35	4	10	0
1978 (D)	31	11	7	−4
1980 (D)	29	15	5	−2
1982 (R)	34	11	4	−4
1984 (R)	26	11	12	0
1986 (R)	28	9	12	−2
1988 (R)	30	7	12	−2
1990 (R)	31	4	14	−3
			Average change =	−2.32

Source: See Appendix.

Notes: R = Republican, D = Democratic. Nebraska is excluded because its state legislative elections are nonpartisan. Minnesota is excluded from 1946 through 1970 because its state legislative elections were nonpartisan.

we mean the number of states in which the president's party has a majority of seats in both chambers of the legislature. This figure is readily calculated; it parallels the gubernatorial measure; and it has substantive appeal, since the party that controls the legislature influences policy outputs and congressional redistricting.

Table 7.3 displays the partisan makeup of the state legislatures according to this measure, from 1946 to 1990. The number of legislatures that the president's party gained or lost overall in each election is registered in column 4. For example, the −3 for 1990 means that the Republicans had a net loss of 3 state legislatures as a result of the 1990 election. The incumbent party usually fares poorly. On average, it lost control of about 2 legislatures every election. In this way, at least, state legislative elections are no different from congressional and gubernatorial contests: it costs something for the incumbent party to govern.

With incumbent party gains or losses (column 4) serving as our dependent variable (SL) of partisan change in state legislatures, we can now estimate a forecasting model contoured after our congressional results. As before, we begin with indicators tapping the economy, presidential popularity, and exposure. The first two independent variables are measured as they were in the gubernatorial model; however, the exposure measure can be simplified because the number of elections is the same from year to year. Thus, exposure (XL) is counted as the number of states in which the incumbent party controls both legislative chambers going into the election. In 1990, for instance, the exposure term was 7, meaning the Republicans controlled both chambers in 7 states. We expect that the more states are exposed, the worse the incumbent party will do. Applying regression analysis to this initial specification yields the following:

$$SL = -7.68^{*} + 1.54^{*}(E \times M) + .10^{**}PP - 0.07XL \quad \text{(Eq. 7.3)}$$

$$(-1.86) \quad (2.88) \quad (1.50) \quad (-0.6)$$

$R^2 = .44$ Adj. $R^2 = .35$ N = 22
SEE = 3.98 D-W = 2.24

where SL = partisan change in state legislatures; XL = number of state legislatures in which the incumbent party has control of both chambers; *, ** = statistically significant at .05 or .10, respectively, $|t| > 1.73, 1.33$; all other terms and statistics are defined as with equation 7.2.

Again, as we found with the initial gubernatorial model, results are mixed. Economics, the midterm cycle, and presidential approval register statistical significance. However, presidential approval is barely significant at .10. Further, the exposure variable (XL), surprisingly, fails to reach statistical significance at any conventional level. Moreover, the fit statistics are low enough that forecasting would be an error-prone enterprise. The explanation embodied in the equation merits reconsideration, but the paths to theoretical improvement seem, especially in this case, unclear. Therefore, we tested different hypotheses. Trend variables used in our past models were included; these were found to be insignificant, along with the exposure variable. Further, it was found that the independent effects of the economic growth and midterm variables actually outweighed their multiplicative effects. While these findings suggest fruitful avenues for respecification, they fail to capture unique features of the state legislative arena. In that regard, another possibility presented itself. Recall that the state legislatures take the lead in redrawing congressional boundaries every ten years. Thus we constructed a redistricting variable (B) to distinguish elections occurring in a redistricting year (scored 1 for a redistricting year, 0 otherwise). Our hypothesis was that the incumbent party would receive a more or less immediate electoral advantage as a result of its role in redrawing the legislative boundaries.

On the basis of these reflections, we proposed that partisan change in state legislatures was an additive function of four variables: economics, popularity, midterm status, and redistricting. When this revised model is estimated using multiple regression, it yields the following estimates:

$$SL = -13.75* + 1.01*E + 0.12*PP + 5.35*M + 3.83*B \qquad \text{(Eq. 7.4)}$$

$$(-6.21) \quad (3.86) \quad (2.95) \quad (4.95) \quad (3.03)$$

$R^2 = .80$ Adj. $R^2 = .75$ $N = 22$

SEE $= 2.46$ D-W $= 1.91$

where B = a redistricting variable, scored 0 for all years except 1950, 1960, 1970, 1980, and 1990, which are scored 1; * = statistically significant at .05 or more, one-tail, $|t| > 1.74$; all other terms and statistics are defined as with equation 7.3.

This model, which is more developed theoretically, also generates more encouraging statistical results. All the predictor variables are highly significant (at the .05 level or better). Further, the model fits the data well. The coefficients suggest more precisely how particular forces move state legislative elections. The president's party can expect to gain control of 1 additional state legislature for every 1 percent growth in personal income. Further, the incumbent party can anticipate controlling 1 additional legislature for every 8 percentage point rise in presidential approval (that is, $.12 \times 8 = .96$). And the incumbent party can count on controlling approximately 5 more legislatures in presidential, as opposed to midterm, years. Finally, the coefficient for the redistricting variable (B) confirms our hypothesis that the incumbent party does better in redistricting years, garnering almost 4 more legislatures.

The predictive abilities of equation 7.4 are displayed in Table 7.4. Column 3 reports the prediction error. As the APE of 1.68 indicates, the forecasts are very accurate. They never miss the mark by more than 4 legislatures, and in more than half the elections the error is 1 or 0. With prediction error this low, equation 7.4 would seem to merit consideration as a forecasting tool.

Table 7.4 Forecasting Accuracy of the State Legislative Model, 1948-1990

SL = −13.75 + 1.01E + 0.12PP + 5.35M + 3.83B

Year (president's party)	(1) Actual change	(2) Predicted change	(3) Error (1) − (2)
1948 (D)	2	2	0
1950 (D)	0	1	−1
1952 (D)	−3	−4	1
1954 (R)	−6	−7	1
1956 (R)	−2	1	−3
1958 (R)	−11	−7	−4
1960 (R)	8	4	4
1962 (D)	−3	−3	0
1964 (D)	9	5	4
1966 (D)	−9	−7	−2
1968 (D)	−4	−1	−3
1970 (R)	−2	−1	−1
1972 (R)	−1	0	−1
1974 (R)	−12	−13	1
1976 (R)	0	−1	1
1978 (D)	−4	−6	2
1980 (D)	−2	−2	0
1982 (R)	−4	−8	4
1984 (R)	0	0	0
1986 (R)	−2	−3	1
1988 (R)	−2	−1	−1
1990 (R)	−3	−1	−2

Notes: R = Republican, D = Democratic. Column 2 is the actual legislative control change for the incumbent party. Column 3 is the control change predicted from equation 7.4. Column 4 is the prediction error. On the basis of column 3, the average absolute prediction error = 1.68.

Conclusion

We have developed models to predict gubernatorial and state legislative election outcomes. At their core, these equations contain many of the same variables as our presidential and congressional models. For example, all the models have an economic variable and a presidential popularity variable. Also, they all take into consideration the type of election (presidential or midterm). While these similarities are satisfying from a practical perspective, they are also important from a theoretical perspective. Our models suggest that regardless of the electoral arena, the collective choices of the American voter are structured in much the same way. The outcomes of all the elections we have examined—from presidential to state legislative—hinge largely on a few key national factors. This is not to say that unique local and state issues play no role. Indeed, to suggest this would be silly. Local and state issues do influence campaigns, and they are probably one of the major reasons for the error that remains in our models. Still, it is theoretically pleasing that the behavior of the electorate, acting in the aggregate, can be forecast so well by a handful of essentially national variables.

As a final exploration into forecasting, we go outside the United States. We believe that voters in other advanced industrial democracies respond to economic and noneconomic issues by rewarding or punishing the incumbent, in much the same way as American voters do. If so, then accurate forecasting models of aggregate election outcomes should be identifiable for many Western democracies. To illustrate this cross-cultural potential, we pursue the modeling of French national election outcomes in Chapter 8.

Note

1. For example, the Virginia and New Jersey gubernatorial elections, held in 1989, are considered 1990 elections. Otherwise, it would be necessary to incorporate years with only one or two elections into our time series model, which does not seem sensible.

CHAPTER 8

French Elections: President and National Assembly

France, like the United States, is a wealthy industrial democracy, a leader among the nations of the West. However, the political systems of the two countries differ in many ways. Before turning to the issues of election forecasting, we ought to review a few of the pertinent differences. (For a useful introduction to French politics, see Safran 1991.) In the United States, the basic rules of the game, as spelled out by the Constitution, remain the same after two hundred years. France, in contrast, has been governed under sixteen different constitutions since its revolution. Furthermore, French democratic institutions have not infrequently been fundamentally disrupted, suspended, or altered. The current republic, born in 1958, emerged from the leadership crises and parliamentary instability surrounding participation in the European Common Market and decolonization in Algeria. General Charles de Gaulle, who was returned to power to solve these problems, oversaw the passage of the Constitution of the Fifth Republic in September of that year; then he was elected to the presidency.

Under the rules of the Fifth Republic, the government is a presidential parliamentary system. Since 1962, the president has been popularly elected, the majority winner in a second-round ballot for a seven-year term. To direct the government on a day-to-day basis, the president appoints a prime minister, whose tenure depends on the majority approval of the National Assembly, where real legislative power resides in the French system. The Deputies of the National Assembly are popularly elected from single-member districts in a two-round ballot (except in 1986, when the procedure consisted of a single round and proportional representation). There is considerable interest in these elections, with an

Table 8.1 French National Assembly Results, by Party, Popular Vote, First Ballot, 1958-1988

Year	
1958	Communists 19%, Socialists 16%, Radicals 7%, MRP 11%, Modérés 22%, Gaullist 20%, Other 5%
1962	Communists 22%, Socialists 13%, Radicals 8%, MRP 9%, Modérés 10%, RI 4%, Gaullist 32%, Other 2%
1967	Communists 22%, Socialists/Radicals 21%, CD 13%, Modérés 4%, Gaullists/RI 38%, Other 2%
1968	Communists 20%, Socialists/Radicals 16%, Centre PDM 10%, Modérés 2%, Gaullists/RI 46%, Other 6%
1973	Communists 21%, Socialists 19%, Left Radicals 2%, Reform 13%, Gaullists/RI/Modérés 38%, Other 7%
1978	Communists 21%, Socialists 23%, Left Radicals 2%, UDF 21%, Gaullists 23%, Other 10%
1981	Communists 16%, Socialists/Left Radicals 38%, UDF 19%, Gaullists 21%, Other 6%
1986	Communists 10%, Socialists/Left Radicals 31%, UDF 8%, UDF-RPR Joint 21%, Gaullists 11%, National Front 10%, Other 9%
1988	Communists 11%, Socialists/Left Radicals 36%, UDF 18%, RPR 19%, National Front 10%, Other 6%

Sources: 1958-1986 from Michael S. Lewis-Beck and Andrew Skalaban, "The French Electorate: From Change to Change?" In *Electoral Change: Responses to Evolving Social and Attitudinal Structure in Fifteen Countries,* ed. Mark Franklin, Thomas Mackie, and Henry Valen (Cambridge: Cambridge University Press, in press); 1988 is from *Les Elections Legislatives: Dossiers et Documents, June 1988* (Paris: *Le Monde*).

Note: MRP = Mouvement Républicain Populaire; RI = Républicains Indépendants; CD = Centre Démocrate; PDM = Progrès et Démocratie Moderne; UDF = Union pour la Démocratie Française; RPR = Rassemblement pour la République (Gaullist).

average of about 75 percent of eligible voters participating in the first-round ballot. The numerous political parties help keep participation high by offering voters a wide choice, at least by American standards. In Table 8.1 are listed the leading parties, along with their first-ballot popular vote shares in the nine National Assembly elections of the Fifth Republic.

The parties are ordered left to right on an ideological spectrum, running from the Communists on the far left to the National Front on the far right. This wide array of parties, coupled with an active electorate and a history of fragile institutions, results in chronic leadership problems for the French chief executive. Yet the president has generally managed to keep a firm hand on the policy direction of government during the Fifth Republic. The main reason for the president's policy success is the existence of a majority coalition in the National Assembly allied to the president. From de Gaulle (1958-1969) to Pompidou (1969-1974), a Gaullist president could pretty much count on a Gaullist-led majority in the Assembly. Although President Giscard d'Estaing himself (1974-1981) was not a Gaullist, he still managed to command the same traditional right-wing majority in parliament. In 1981, after Socialist Mitterrand defeated Giscard and was elected president, he dissolved the National Assembly. In the ensuing parliamentary elections, the voters gave his party an absolute majority, thus enabling him to launch his Socialist legislative program.

President Mitterrand kept executive policy initiative firmly in his hands until the 1986 National Assembly elections, when he lost his majority to the rightist parties. (The Gaullist RPR won 158 seats, the Giscardian UDF captured 132.) As president, his duty was to appoint the prime minister; however, no Socialist would be accepted by the rightist majority. Therefore, he selected Jacques Chirac, mayor of Paris and head of the Gaullist RPR. As it evolved, Prime Minister Chirac demonstrated that he exercised the more effective control over domestic policy legislation. Thus, French executive power became divided between a president of one party and a prime minister of another. Fortunately for President Mitterrand, this period of "cohabitation" came to an end in 1988. He was reelected president and, in the legislative contest, the RPR-UDF coalition on the right lost its majority. With the appointment of a likeminded prime minister (Socialist Michel Rocard), President Mitterrand appeared once again able to set the course of French public policy, foreign and domestic. (In May 1991, Rocard resigned and Mitterrand appointed Socialist Edith Cresson to replace him.)

After this introduction, even the most enthusiastic election forecasters might feel that the French case is their Waterloo. It seems so complicated, compared with the U.S. case. There are two chief executives (president and prime minister), five or six major parties (covering the entire left-right ideological spectrum), shifting coalitions (in parliament and out), elections held at irregular times (some near the presidential contest, some not), changing voting rules (one or two rounds, proportional or not), to name a few complications. What of all this, exactly, does one want to forecast? Can incumbent party strength (or its lack) be forecasted, as in the U.S. case? Yes. We will show how, looking first at presidential elections, then at National Assembly elections and, finally, at the two together.

Presidential Elections

According to the rules of the Fifth Republic, as they now stand, the voters choose the president in a majority system with a two-round ballot. If no candidate obtains a majority on the first ballot, then there is a runoff between the top two. In fact, in every presidential election of the

Table 8.2 Fifth Republic Presidential Election Results, Second Ballot, 1965-1988

Year	Incumbent candidate[a]	Incumbent vote share	Opposition candidate	Opposition vote share
1965	de Gaulle	54.5%	Mitterrand	45.5%
1969	Pompidou	57.6	Poher	42.5
1974	Giscard d'Estaing	50.7	Mitterrand	49.4
1981	Giscard d'Estaing	48.2	Mitterrand	51.8
1988	Mitterrand	54.0	Chirac	46.0

Source: See Appendix.

[a]The candidate of the incumbent party (or party coalition).

Fifth Republic, the winning candidate (listed in Table 8.2) has achieved his majority on the second ballot.

Although five elections is not a great number, interesting changes have occurred. First, incumbents are not always reelected, as Giscard's 1981 loss to Mitterrand makes clear. Second, there is *alternance* ("alternation"), as the French call it, in power. That is, one party, or one party coalition, does not always win. However, this capacity for alternating party control was not demonstrated until 1981, when the right-wing rule begun by de Gaulle in 1958 came to an end with the Socialist victory of Mitterrand. These two characteristics—the vulnerability of incumbents and alternation in party control—the French presidency shares with the American presidency.

Are the forces that brought about these changing presidential election results also similar from one country to the other? Almost no aggregate time series research has been done on the determinants of the popular vote for the French president. But, luckily, considerable research of this type exists on the determinants of French presidential popularity (in English, see Hibbs and Vasilatos 1981; Lafay 1985; Lewis-Beck 1980b). As in the United States, changing macroeconomic conditions influence the president's approval level in the public opinion polls. Specifically, bad economic conditions (rising unemployment, accelerating inflation, deteriorating income, slow growth) harm the president's rating. Therefore, perhaps bad economic conditions can be shown to lead directly to vote losses for the president and his party. We will test this hypothesis.

Since there are only five elections to study, we have to keep things simple. Let us naively suppose that macroeconomic change entirely determines French presidential election winners. In other words, under good economic performance, the incumbent (party or party coalition) candidate wins reelection. However, under bad economic performance, the incumbent loses. We see that this simple rule seems to work. When Giscard lost in 1981 (with 48.2 percent), he had helped compile the worst economic record of any Fifth Republic president: the unemployment rate stood at 7 percent, the inflation rate at 14 percent, the economic growth rate at less than 1 percent. In contrast, Pompidou, who won in 1969 with the largest margin (57.6 percent), had enjoyed a booming annual economic growth rate of more than 7 percent.

In general, all five elections fit this pattern nicely, if we risk an experiment and put the tiny number of cases into a bivariate regression equation. Here is the popular vote for the incumbent (FV), predicted from the annual economic growth rate (FG):

$$FV = 47.13* + 1.29*FG \qquad \text{(Eq. 8.1)}$$

$$(37.39) \qquad (5.23)$$

$R^2 = .90$ Adj. $R^2 = .87$ $N = 5$
SEE = 1.31   D-W = 2.01

where FV = popular vote percentage, second-round ballot for the incumbent president (or his party coalition candidate); FG = annual growth rate for real GDP (gross domestic product, the European equivalent to GNP) in the election year; the figures in parentheses are the t-ratios; * = statistically significant at .05 or better, one-tail, $|t| > 2.35$; R^2 = coefficient of determination; adj. R^2 = adjusted coefficient of determination; SEE = standard error of estimate; D-W = Durbin-Watson statistic; N = the five presidential elections of the Fifth Republic (1965, 1969, 1974, 1981, and 1988); see Appendix for data sources.

As the R-squared indicates, almost all (90 percent) of the variation in presidential vote can be accounted for by fluctuations in economic growth. The scatterplot in Figure 8.1, with the regression line fitted to the five points, dramatizes the strength of this relationship. As in the United States, macroeconomic conditions appear to be highly predictive of presidential vote. Moreover, individual-level election survey research reported elsewhere suggests that the implied economic voting relationship is not spurious (Lewis-Beck 1988b, 72-74). In addition, the surveys reveal that French citizens do consider noneconomic issues as well. For example, the issues of ecology, nuclear energy, crime, abortion, immigration, military spending, and European unity are each significantly correlated with vote intention in France.

Thus, to arrive at a satisfactory forecasting model, we need to find a good national level indicator of such issues. Taking a cue from our American work (Chapter 2), we contend that presidential popularity taps

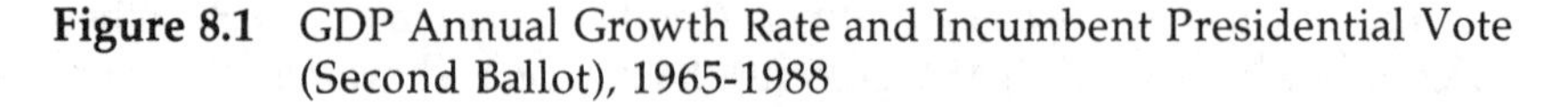

Figure 8.1 GDP Annual Growth Rate and Incumbent Presidential Vote (Second Ballot), 1965-1988

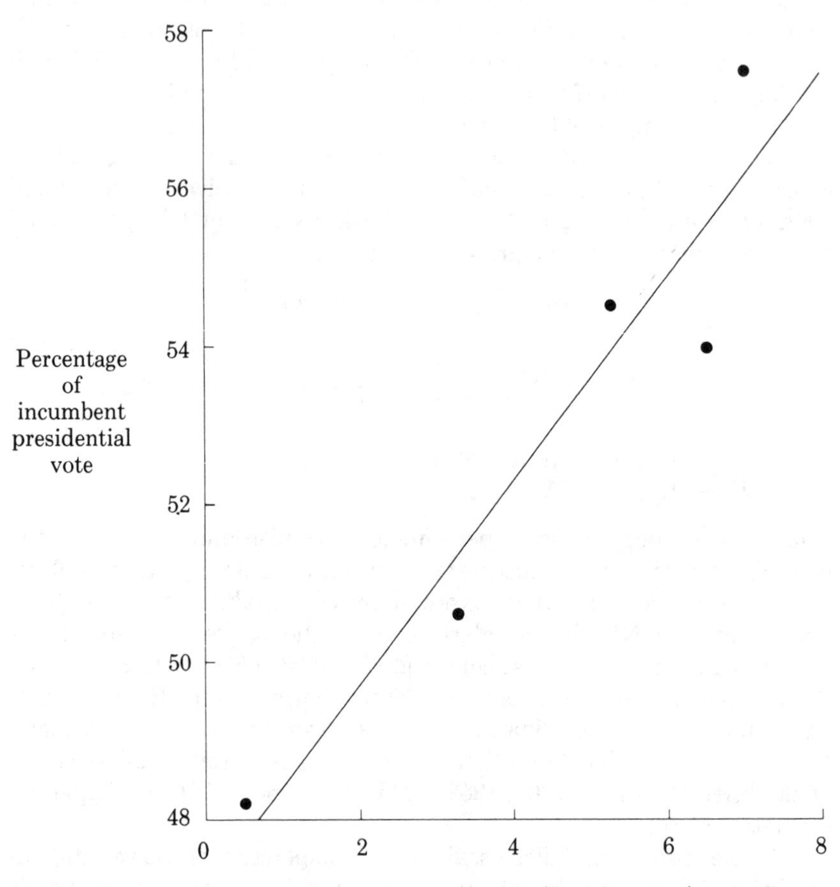

voter sentiment on these noneconomic issues. In France a major polling organization, IFOP (*Institut Français d' Opinion Publique*), regularly poses a Gallup-type approval item to a national sample: "Are you satisfied or dissatisfied with [*name*] as president of the republic?" To the extent that respondents are happy about the president's handling of social, cultural, and foreign policy matters (like those listed above), we would expect the "satisfied" answers to increase. In turn, the increased satisfaction should translate into more votes for the president. This appears to be the case. When presidential popularity (measured as percent satisfied in the IFOP poll) from the month nearest the presidential election is correlated with incumbent popular vote, r = .68.

Table 8.3 Correlations (r) of Selected Presidential Popularity and GDP Growth Indicators (at Different Lags) with Presidential Vote

	Presidential vote
Presidential popularity	
Time (t)	.68
Time (t − 6)	.77
GDP growth	
time (t)	.95
time (t − 6,9)	.79
time (t − 12,24)	.57

Source: See Appendix.

Notes: Presidential vote is second-round percentage for incumbent president (or his coalition candidate). Popularity is percent satisfied in IFOP (*Institut Français d' Opinion Publique*) poll (t = nearest to election; t − 6 = six months before election). GDP growth is percent growth rate for real GDP (t = year of the election; t − 6,9 = quarter falling six months before the election; t − 12,24 = year before the election).

Thus far, two familiar variables—economic growth and presidential popularity—seem to be good candidates for a forecasting model. However, several problems remain to be solved. First, with only five elections, we cannot really get away with putting two independent variables in one equation. (Technically, we would be stacking the deck in our favor by exhausting the degrees of freedom.) Second, the two variables, as measured, are correlated .82, meaning that empirically they are so much alike that separate effects will be difficult to untangle. (Technically speaking, we have a multicollinearity problem.) Third, and most important, the two variables are essentially measured at the time of the election itself, meaning there is no lead time; without that, of course, forecasting is impossible.

In Table 8.3 we experiment with different past time points for these popularity and GDP variables, correlating each with presidential vote. A few points stand out. As with the U.S. case, popularity measured six months before the election correlates higher (r = .77) than popularity measured at election time. Popularity assessed at a certain distance, before the battle heats up, predicts more accurately. Turning to the economic growth variable, one also observes that the preferred lag for GDP is the quarter at a six-month distance, with r = .79. These strong lagged correlations suggest the potential for aggregate forecasting of French election outcomes. However, before multivariate analysis can be carried out, a larger sample size is necessary. Therefore, we turn to consideration of results from National Assembly contests, which almost doubles the number of available national election observations.

National Assembly Elections

Our discussion so far has led to a straightforward theory of French voter choice: favor (oppose) the incumbent when, on balance, one is satisfied (dissatisfied) on economic and noneconomic issues. What does this choice mean when applied specifically to National Assembly elections? The meaning lies in the terms *incumbent* and *opposition*. Recall that, for the U.S. House of Representatives (Chapter 4), we followed the prevailing custom of defining the incumbent by the party of the president. We employ the same strategy here. The incumbent party (or party coalition) in the National Assembly is that of the president. Thus, for example, going into the 1967 Assembly elections, there was a Gaullist-led incumbent party coalition opposed by Socialists, Communists, and other leftist parties. The legislative vote choice, then, can be reduced to two: an incumbent party or an opposition party.

In the actual analysis, it is preferable to emphasize the opposition side of this dichotomy, since the opposition is a more coherent concept than incumbency in French politics. Throughout most of the Fifth Republic the leftist block, with its more cohesive Communist-Socialist core, has been the opposition. The rightist block of parties has been more fluid, and has only relatively recently been in opposition. So defined, opposition voting in the nine National Assembly elections of the Fifth Republic correlates, as the issues theory predicts, with our economic growth and presidential popularity variables. For instance, take the first-ballot percentage of votes for all opposition parties. (Because of changing election rules, we begin by examining popular vote shares, rather than seats. Also, the first-ballot more accurately reveals voter preference.) If, under deteriorating economic conditions, voters break away from incumbent parties and turn to the opposition, then the data ought to show that. In fact, the GDP growth measure is correlated −.64 with percentage support for opposition parties. Furthermore, heightened dissatisfaction with the president's handling of noneconomic issues should, as well, relate to an increase in opposition voting. Indeed, presidential approval is correlated −.80 with popular vote support for opposition parties. This rather strong relationship, between popularity and opposition vote, is depicted in the scatterplot of Figure 8.2.

GDP growth and presidential popularity should be examined together in a multiple regression model of National Assembly voting. Before we do that, however, the model needs to be filled out. The dependent variable here is simple vote share (that is, a percentage, not a *change* in percentage). Of course, from one election to the next, many voters will not change. They will simply vote the same party, completely ignoring the issues. In the United States, we attribute this habit to party identification. In France, this partisan phenomenon operates basically as

Figure 8.2 Presidential Popularity (Lagged Six Months) and Opposition Parties Vote in National Assembly Elections (First Ballot), 1958-1988

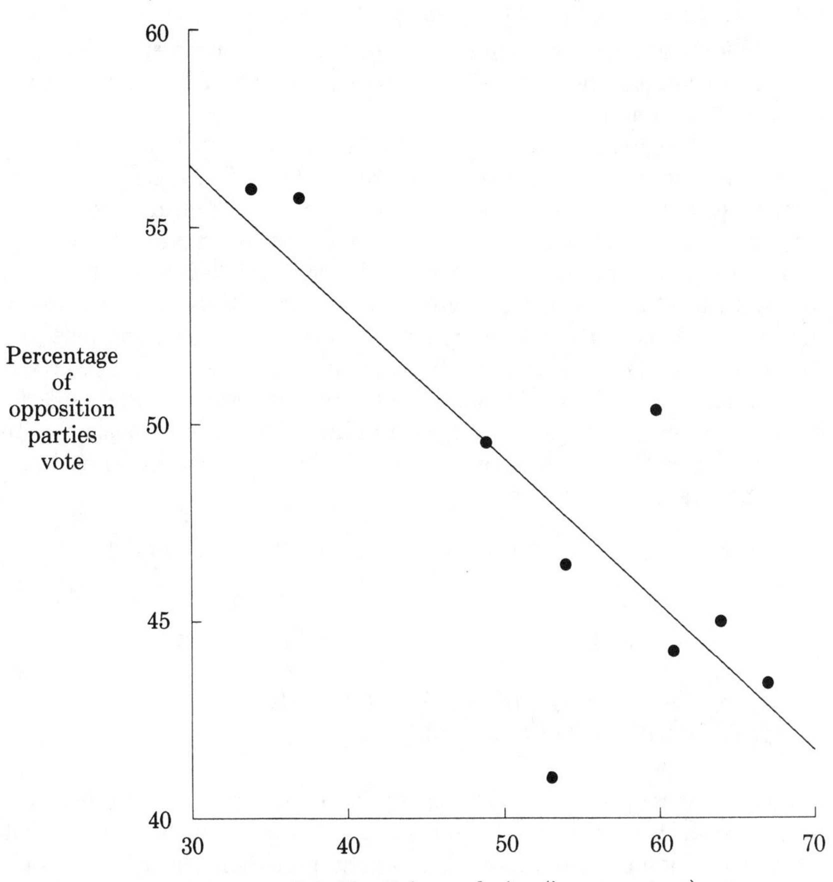

attachment to an ideology: left, center, or right (see Lewis-Beck 1983, 1984; Lewis-Beck and Skalaban in press). Most French citizens (close to 90 percent) express an ideology when asked to, and most consistently locate themselves at the center or on the right. Furthermore, on average, only a minority of the French electorate actually votes left, as the average vote support for all leftist parties is 46.5 percent (first-ballot, 1958-1988 legislative elections).

How can the ideology variable be incorporated effectively into an aggregate time series model? The problem is made difficult by the stability of ideological identification across time in France (Lewis-Beck 1984; Lewis-Beck and Skalaban in press). When almost everyone has an ideology that seldom changes, then ideology has little effect on changing the nationwide vote total. However, little change does not mean no change. One shift is the recent hike in votes for the left, beginning with Mitterrand's victory in 1981. Nevertheless, the full electoral effect of Mitterand (and Socialist) gains becomes somewhat blunted in National Assembly contests, because of the minority status of leftist ideological identification among the voters.

In other words, Mitterrand's coattails do not stretch as far as they might because of the majority center-right ideological resistance in the electorate. A practical implication is that when the presidential incumbent is on the left, opposition voting in Assembly races will increase. (Cases in point include the 1986 and 1988 legislative results.) The complexities of this ideological interplay, as it manifests itself nationally, can be modeled with a simple dichotomous variable measuring partisanship of the president (whether the president is from a left-wing party or not). Thus the following National Assembly regression model suggests itself, with popular vote share determined by issues (measured by economic growth and presidential popularity) and partisanship (measured by the president's party):

$$NA = \underset{(8.27)}{59.63^{*}} - \underset{(1.16)}{0.19^{***}}FP - \underset{(1.00)}{3.08}FG + \underset{(1.86)}{5.28^{**}}PL \qquad \text{(Eq. 8.2)}$$

$R^2 = .79$ Adj. $R^2 = .67$ $N = 9$
SEE $= 3.08$ D-W $= 2.33$

where NA = opposition popular vote share percentage in the National Assembly election (that is, the percentage of total votes on the first ballot for parties opposed to the incumbent president's legislative coalition); FP = presidential popularity six months before the election; FG = GDP real growth rate in the quarter six months before the election; PL = partisanship (1 if the president is from a left-wing party, 0 otherwise); *, **, *** = statistically significant at .05, .10, or .15, respectively, one-tail, $|t| > 2.02, 1.48, 1.16$, respectively; N = the nine legislative elections of the Fifth Republic; other statistics are defined as with equation 8.1; data sources are in the Appendix.

The direction of the estimated regression coefficients supports the proposed explanation. As economic growth increases, opposition voting in National Assembly elections decreases. Further, the more popular the president is, the less support there is for the parties opposing him. With regard to the third independent variable, partisanship, we observe, as expected, that a leftist president generates more opposition voting in Assembly contests. The three variables together seem to have a fair amount of prediction potential, accounting for more than 70 percent of the variation in vote share. Before we move into the forecasting arena, however, we must forge another link. Because of changing election laws, the preferred dependent variable in equation 8.2 is votes, not seats. Still, real party power in the Assembly ultimately rests with seat—not vote—totals. Therefore, an important question is how closely they are tied. Here is the simple regression of actual Assembly seats on our popular vote measure:

$$NS = -585.92* + 16.45*NA \qquad \text{(Eq. 8.3)}$$

$$(6.87) \qquad (9.30)$$

$R^2 = .925$ Adj. $R^2 = .91$ $N = 9$
SEE = 26.65 D-W = 1.60

where NS = number of National Assembly seats won by parties in opposition to the president; NA = opposition vote percentage (of first-ballot votes for the parties in opposition to the president); * = statistically significant at .05 or better, one-tail, $|t| > 2.35$; the statistics and data sources are defined as with equation 8.2.

According to equation 8.3, there is, in fact, an almost perfect linear relationship (R^2 = .925) between seats and votes in the French National Assembly elections. How well one predicts the other is shown graphically in the scatterplot of Figure 8.3. First-ballot voting preferences, at least in the aggregate, essentially determine the distribution of party power in the Assembly itself. Hence, forecasting a popular vote outcome poses little difficulty. On the contrary, the popular vote measure is advantageous, for it can easily be integrated into a larger model of French national elections, as we will show.

A Unified Model for French National Elections

The Fifth Republic has been in existence only since 1958. Since that time, there have been only a few national elections—five presidential and nine National Assembly. For our U.S. study we were able to examine eleven presidential and twenty-two House of Representatives contests. Obviously, the small sample of French elections, interesting as they are, presents a problem. With few elections, we have less confidence in our results. (For example, in our equations, the tiny samples can make the attainment of statistical significance difficult.) How can we expand our data base, thereby making our forecasts more secure? We could wait for other elections to occur, then incorporate these new results into our

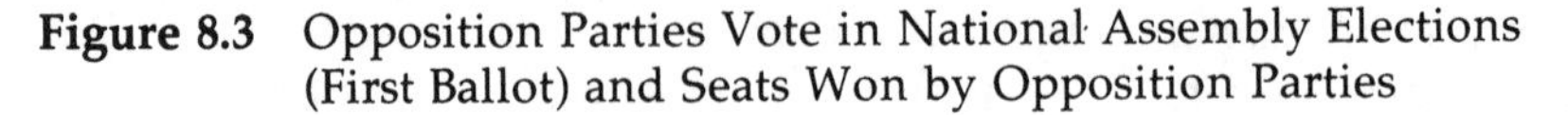

Figure 8.3 Opposition Parties Vote in National Assembly Elections (First Ballot) and Seats Won by Opposition Parties

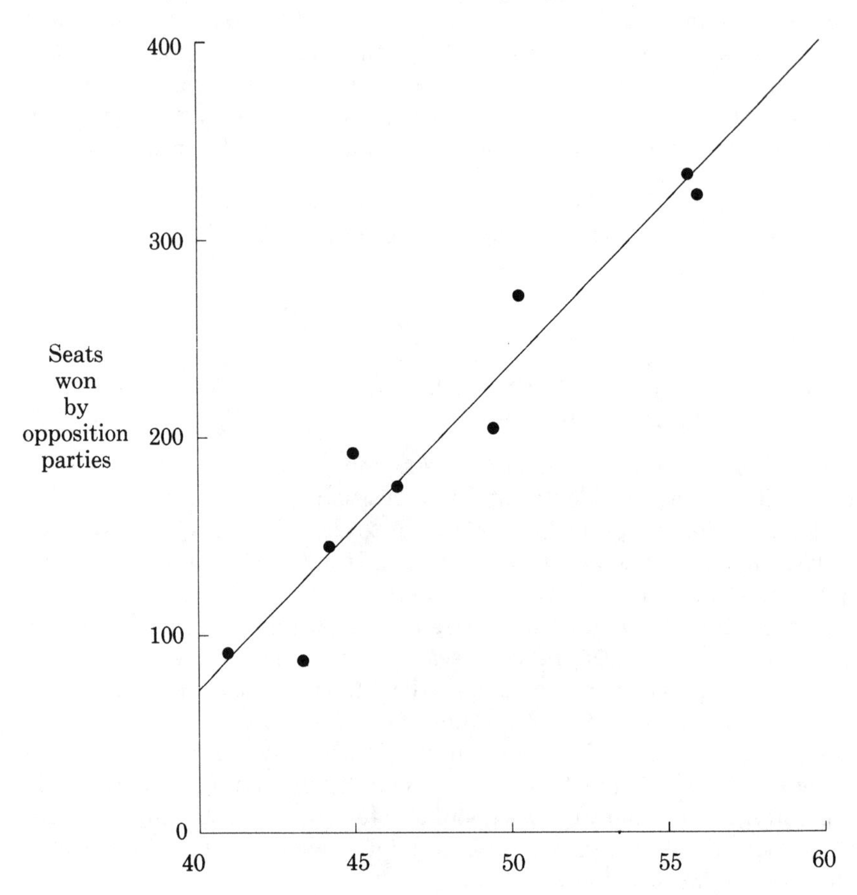

models. Or, in the meantime, we can combine data from the two election arenas into one model.

A combination strategy makes sense since we believe that, in the main, the forces that move the French voter are similar in presidential and National Assembly elections. The president is the active decision focus of the French voter. When considering an issue, the French citizen asks how the president—and the party coalition the president commands—is handling it. If the incumbent coalition is judged to be doing a bad job, either in the presidency or in the parliament, then the opposition is favored. Of course, such evaluations do not totally determine choice. Some voters are swayed by partisanship, blindly sticking with the right (or perhaps the left) regardless of issues. In other words, in French national elections the following simple theory might explain an anti-incumbent, pro-opposition vote:

$$\text{Vote} = \begin{matrix}\text{Economic}\\ \text{issues}\end{matrix} + \begin{matrix}\text{Noneconomic}\\ \text{issues}\end{matrix} + \text{Partisanship} \quad \text{(Eq. 8.4)}$$

Suppose we combine the presidential and Assembly observations into one enlarged data set and estimate this theoretical model, using the independent variables already measured (GDP growth, presidential popularity, and incumbent party):

$$\underset{}{O} = \underset{(10.60)}{62.87*} - \underset{(1.97)}{0.26*FP} - \underset{(1.04)}{1.99\dagger FG} + \underset{(1.47)}{2.99**PL} \quad \text{(Eq. 8.5)}$$

$R^2 = .71$ Adj. $R^2 = .62$ $N = 14$
SEE $= 2.88$ D-W $= 1.73$

where O = percentage of votes against the president or a party in his coalition (that is, in a second-round presidential election, the popular vote share against the president or his coalition candidate, which is simply the dependent variable of equation 8.1 subtracted from 100; in a National Assembly election, first-round votes for parties opposed to the president's parliamentary coalition, as measured in equation 8.2); *, ** = statistically significant at .05, .10, respectively, one-tail, $|t| > 1.81, 1.37$, respectively; † just misses statistical significance at .15, one-tail, $|t| > 1.09$; other variables, statistics, and data sources are defined as with equations 8.1 and 8.2.

These results, based on a more secure sample of fourteen, give support to our theory of French national elections. Bad economic times favor the opposition, as does declining presidential popularity. Besides, the presence of a leftist in the presidency can heighten opposition support. Moreover, the findings could neither be improved upon nor undercut by the addition of alternative independent variables—namely, measures on "cohabitation," opposition seat support in the past election, election type (presidential or legislative), or the 1986 election rule change to proportional representation.

What does the combined model promise, in terms of forecasting? According to the R-squared, most of the variation in vote support (about 70 percent) can still be accounted for. Further, the standard error of estimate (SEE = 2.88) is below that of the National Assembly model by itself. Thus, as suspected, including the two types of elections improves forecasting prospects. Indeed, the prediction error within the sample of

Table 8.4 Prediction Results from the French National Elections Model

$$O = 62.87 - 0.26FP - 1.99FG + 2.99PL$$

Year/ election[a] (presidential party type)[b]	(1) Actual opposition share[c]	(2) Predicted opposition share	(3) Prediction error (1) − (2)	(4) Correct prediction of winner?
1958/A (right)	43.40%	44.12%	−.72	yes
1962/A (right)	44.2	43.80	.40	yes
1965/P (right)	45.5	44.12	1.38	yes
1967/A (right)	45.0	44.20	.80	yes
1968/A (right)	41.0	47.28	−6.28	yes
1969/P (right)	42.5	44.72	−2.22	yes
1973/A (right)	46.4	46.74	−.34	yes
1974/P (right)	49.4	45.37	4.03	yes
1978/A (right)	49.5	48.75	.75	yes
1981/P (right)	51.8	51.51	.29	yes
1981/A (right)	55.7	53.81	1.89	yes
1986/A (left)	56.0	56.49	−.49	yes
1988/P (left)	46.0	48.42	−2.42	yes
1988/A (left)	50.3	47.39	2.91	yes

Sources: See Appendix.

[a]A = Assembly; P = presidential.

[b]Presidential party, labeled right or left: right for de Gaulle (1958-1969), Pompidou (1969-1974), and Giscard d'Estaing (1974-1981); left for Mitterrand (1981-1988).

[c]Opposition vote share for presidential elections is the loser's percentage on the second ballot. For National Assembly elections, it is the percentage of first-ballot votes going to presidential opposition parties (i.e., for 1958-1981 essentially leftist parties, for 1986-1988 essentially rightist parties). In particular, here are the opposition parties for each contest: 1958 = Communists, Union des Forces Démocratiques, SFIO, radicals; 1962 = Communists, Extrême-Gauche, SFIO, radicals; 1967 = Communists, Socialists, Extrême-Gauche, PSU, Fédération de la Gauche, Divers Gauche; 1968 = Communists, Socialists, PSU, Fédération de la Gauche, Divers Gauche; 1973 = Communists, Extrême-Gauche, PSU, Socialists, Divers Gauche, Radicaux de Gauche; 1978 = Communists, Socialists, Mouvement des Radicaux de Gauche, Extrême-Gauche, Divers Gauche; 1981 = Communists, Socialists, Mouvement des Radicaux de Gauche, Divers Gauche; 1986, 1988 = Union pour la Démocratie Française, Rassemblement pour la République, Front National, Divers Droit.

elections themselves (the APE) is only 1.78. In other words, on average, the popular vote shares in these Fifth Republic elections are predicted with less than 2 percent error.

That is a fair degree of accuracy, and it compares favorably with our U.S. popular vote results (see Chapter 3). But in a system as apparently volatile as the French one, it is important to ask whether this degree of accuracy is enough. Specifically, does it correctly foretell the critical swings of electoral fortune from opposition to governing status and back?

An answer appears in Table 8.4 (see column 4). Assume the following prediction rules for the model: if it predicts that the opposition vote share is greater than 50 percent, then the opposition should win; if it predicts less than 50 percent, however, the opposition should lose.

By these rules, how well does the model predict? It is correct every time. Note, for example, that for the elections from 1958 to 1978, it would always accurately predict the opposition's loss. Of course, after that period, there were major switches. Still, it works. First, the watershed victory of Mitterrand in 1981 could be predicted, as could be the subsequent leftist triumph in the National Assembly. Then, in 1986, the model picks up the switch back to the right. Last, it calls for the return to power of Mitterrand and the Socialists in 1988, which is what happened.

Conclusion

The French political system is in many ways different from that of the United States. Under the Fifth Republic, we observe multiple parties, from the extreme left to the extreme right, each competing for power. A participative mass electorate intensifies the competition, while changing election rules seem to make the outcome uncertain. The dual executive, president and prime minister, poses further threats to stability. Nevertheless, for all these elements of difference, the election results themselves can be forecast, much as in the United States. From a national perspective, the French voter appears to reward or punish the incumbent for good or bad performance on the issues. These shifting evaluations of the issues (as measured by GDP and popularity), taken in conjunction with underlying partisan attachments, allow the accurate forecasting of outcomes in presidential and National Assembly contests.

CHAPTER 9

Models Applied: Forecasting the Next Election

The confirmation of a forecasting model's usefulness comes in its application to a forthcoming election. Figuring out how a model worked the day after the election rewards us with too little, too late. As forecasters, we make the calculations and announce our predictions well in advance. This is perhaps the most demanding rule of the forecasting game, but it keeps competition fair and lively. Going public with an election call forces a modeler to give special attention to the possible defects of his or her own model. For example, with the aid of an earlier model for presidential races, we made before-election forecasts for the 1984 and 1988 contests (Lewis-Beck and Rice 1984; Lewis-Beck 1985). Neither ex ante prediction was flatly wrong, in that both correctly foresaw the winner (Reagan and Bush, respectively). However, the percentage and pattern of error called for revisions, which finally led to the current model (Chapter 3). When prediction errors fall beyond the expected range, a forecaster rethinks the explanation, perhaps introducing theoretical improvement. (By way of analogy, imagine how an astrophysicist may rethink the specification of trajectory equations when a satellite mysteriously falls out of orbit.) Thus, the judicious election forecaster, by making thoughtful adjustments to a model on the basis of observed error, moves political science closer to a full explanation of electoral outcomes.

Nevertheless, this chapter is not about theory or explanation, statistics or analysis. We have had our say on these matters. Rather, it is a simple user's guide to models already presented, reviewing the arithmetic necessary to forecast an upcoming election. In the United States, the next national elections to be forecast occur in 1992. As we write in 1991, it is impossible to know exactly what our models will forecast. Their lead time, while long, still does not permit definitive forecasts until the summer of 1992. Nevertheless, this current uncertainty has pedagogical advantages, for it permits a quantitative assessment of the impact of different election scenarios. What are the implications of various possible preelection circumstances? Our answer comes from spelling out the electoral consequences of different scores on our predictor variables. For instance, assuming President Bush seeks reelection, how many electoral votes will he lose if the economy moves from boom to bust? By working through such scenarios, we gain a deeper appreciation of how the causal mechanisms underlying the models operate.

We will focus on the U.S. national election arenas that the reader is most likely to want to forecast: for the president, the House, and the Senate. For each, we calculate different scenarios, always applying the relevant equation to the question, Who will win the next election? We begin with the president.

Forecasting the Next Presidential Election

In our final presidential model (equation 3.5) electoral college vote (V) is predicted from four variables: presidential popularity (PP), GNP growth (G), party strength in the House (PS), and candidate strength in the primaries (C). The prediction equation reads as follows:

$$V = 6.83 + 0.86PP + 7.76G + 0.52PS + 19.66C \quad \text{(Eq. 9.1)}$$

where V = percentage of electoral vote for candidate of the president's party; PP = percent who approve of how the president is handling his job, in July of the election year Gallup Poll; G = percentage change in real GNP from fourth quarter of the year before the election to second quarter of the election year; PS = number of House seats the president's party lost in the last election; C = support for presidential party candidate in the primaries (if candidate receives more than 60 percent of all votes cast then scored 1 for strong support, otherwise scored 0).

To apply the equation to the next presidential contest, we first need to ascertain scores on the four independent variables. Even though the 1992 contest is some distance away as of this writing, we know the value of one variable: PS = − 8 (the net number of House seats the Republicans lost in the 1990 election). The values on other variables remain unknown. However, let us make the reasonable suppositions that Bush is again the Republican candidate and that he does well in the primaries; then C = 1. Let us fix these two variables, PS and C, at these scores (− 8 and 1, respectively), and experiment with different possible scenarios regarding the other two variables, popularity and growth.

Table 9.1 Presidential Election Forecasts (Share of Electoral College Vote, 1992), Under Different Popularity and Economic Conditions

$$V = 6.83 + .86PP + 7.76G + 0.52(-8) + 19.66(1)$$

	Presidential popularity (PP)		
Economic growth (G)	40%	50%	60%
− 1%	48.5%	57.1%	65.1%
+ 1%	64.0	72.6	81.2
+ 2%	71.8	80.4	89.0

Notes: Two variables for 1992 are presumed to have known scores; these are set at PS = −8 (net Republican seats lost in House in 1990) and C = 1 (assumes Bush is candidate and does well in primaries, getting more than 60 percent of the total primary vote). The other two variables, PP (presidential popularity in the July 1992 Gallup Poll) and G (GNP growth rate from fourth quarter of 1991 to second quarter of 1992), are presumed unknown. Therefore, each is set at three different possible values, which are plugged into the prediction equation to generate the forecasts.

In Table 9.1, we explore three scenarios for these two variables: good performance, average performance, and poor performance. For presidential popularity, we can use approval scores of 60 percent, 50 percent, and 40 percent. For economic growth, we use scores of −1 percent, + 1 percent, and + 2 percent. Given the other parameter values, the chances of reelection for incumbent Bush are great if he registers a good performance on both popularity and growth (that is, 60 percent and 2 percent, respectively). Under this best case scenario, a landslide victory is forecast, with Bush receiving 89 percent of the electoral vote:

$$\begin{aligned} V &= 6.83 + 0.86(60) + 7.76(2) + 0.52(-8) + 19.66(1) \\ &= 6.83 + 51.6 + 15.52 - 4.16 + 19.66 \\ &= 89.45\% \\ &= 481 \text{ electoral votes (out of 538 total)} \end{aligned}$$

Obviously, the best case might not happen. The worst case scenario is bad performance on both presidential approval and the economy (scores of 40 percent and −1 percent, respectively). In this situation, the model forecasts a loss for Bush, who would be expected to garner only 48.5 percent of the electoral vote. (In between these best and worst case extremes, the different combinations of popularity and growth forecast different outcomes, as Table 9.1 records.)

Thus, even assuming that President Bush runs for reelection, he does not have victory guaranteed. Any presidential campaigner has a chance of losing, however small. The worst case scenario suggests how Bush might meet defeat, even if his party shows well in the House and if he does well in the primaries (that is, PS = −8, C = 1).

Of course, this scenario may not unfold. The values plugged in there need not come to pass. And, as can be seen from Table 9.1, less bleak scenarios spell a Bush win. As another example, suppose we take current (December 1991) values on presidential approval (47 percent) and economic growth (.00, first quarter to third quarter 1991). Substituting these values into equation 9.1, along with the established PS and C scores, yields a forecast of 62.75 percent of the electoral vote. If these current values hold, the model would forecast a Bush reelection in a very close race (with a margin most comparable to Truman's narrow victory in 1948). As we write (almost a year before the election), it is obviously not safe to say that these values will hold. The prudent presidential forecaster must wait until midsummer 1992 when the actual numbers for these variables will be available. (On data sources, see the Appendix.)

Forecasting the Next House Election

The litmus test for a forecasting model is the accuracy of its before-election predictions. Our House model (Chapter 4) has already been so applied (see Michael Oreskes, *New York Times*, September 2, 1990, 10Y). In the summer of 1990, the model forecasted an upcoming net loss of 18 seats for the incumbent Republicans. This forecast turned out close, in a statistical sense, to the 8-seat loss the Republicans in fact experienced that fall. Indeed, the error of 10 seats falls almost exactly at the model's standard error of estimate (of about 10 seats). Furthermore, in substantive terms, the −18 forecast proclaimed that the incumbent party would have a good year (that is, below average midterm losses), which is what happened. Overall, then, the model promises a reasonable performance for the 1992 election.

The House forecasting model (equation 4.3) is based on five variables: income growth (E), midterm or not (M), presidential popularity (PP), presidential party seats exposed (X), and presidential party time in office (T). Here is the prediction equation:

$$HC = -24.43 + 1.70E + 7.54(E \times M) + 0.53PP - 0.65X - 7.14T \qquad \text{(Eq. 9.2)}$$

where HC = number of seats gained or lost by the president's party; E = growth rate in real disposable income from the fourth quarter in the year before the election to the second quarter of the election year; M = a dichotomous variable scored 0 for midterm election year, 1 for presidential election year; PP = the percent approving of the presi-

Table 9.2 House Election Forecasts (Change in Incumbent Seats, 1992), Under Different Popularity and Economic Conditions

$$HC = -24.43 + 1.70E + 7.54(E \times 1) + .53PP - .65(-10) - 7.14(4)$$

	Presidential popularity (PP)		
Economic growth (E)	40%	50%	60%
− 1%	−34.53	−29.23	−23.93
+ 1%	−16.05	−10.75	−5.45
+ 2%	−6.81	−1.51	3.79

Notes: Three variables for 1992 have known scores, set at M = 1 (presidential election year); X = −10 (Republican seats exposed); T = 4 (Republicans in White House more than two terms). The other two variables, PP (presidential popularity the June 1992 Gallup Poll) and E (income growth rate from the fourth quarter in the year before the election to the second quarter of the election year), are presumed unknown. Therefore, each is set at three different possible values, which are plugged into the prediction equation to generate the forecasts.

dent's job handling in the June Gallup Poll of the election year; X = number of seats the president's party has exposed, calculated by taking the average number of seats the president's party held (1948-1990) from the number of seats the president's party held going into the election; T = a counter variable for the length of time the president's party has been in the White House, with 1 = first midterm election (after a change in party control of the presidency), 2 = year of a party's first reelection bid; 3 = the second midterm election year (after a party has won the presidency for the second time); 4 = elections in which a party has controlled the presidency for two or more terms.

Applied to 1992, the equation simplifies quickly, because three out of the five independent variable scores are already known, namely M = 1 (presidential election year); X = −10 Republican seats exposed (average Republican seats held across the 1948-1990 period, 177, subtracted from the actual number of Republican seats held going into the 1992 election, 167); T = 4 (Republicans have been in the White House at least two terms). As can be seen from the equation below, only the economy (E) and popularity (PP) variables remain unknown:

$$HC = -24.43 + 1.70E + 7.54(E \times 1) + .53PP - 0.65(-10) - 7.14(4)$$

Suppose we work through different scenarios for the economy and popularity variables, much as we did for presidential election forecasting in 1992. Here is a worst case scenario forecast, given the known values on M, X, and T and assuming bad performance on the two unknowns; that is, presidential popularity (PP) is low at 40 percent and income growth (E) is at −1 percent:

$$\begin{aligned} HC &= -24.43 + 1.70(-1) + 7.54(-1) + 0.53(40) - .65(-10) - 7.14(4) \\ &= -24.43 - 1.70 - 7.54 + 21.2 + 6.5 - 28.56 \\ &= -34.53 \text{ seats} \end{aligned}$$

According to this worst case scenario, the Republicans would lose 34 or 35 seats, giving them their worst defeat in the House since 1974, when in the aftermath of Watergate they lost 48 seats. Table 9.2 depicts other combinations, yielding other, less disastrous, scenarios. By obtaining the actual values on these critical variables, readers can assess for themselves which scenario turns out to be more accurate.

Forecasting the Next Senate Election

As observed, compared with the House, the Senate has been subjected to much less scrutiny from scholarly forecasters. This is unfortunate, for the Senate has shown itself more capable of actual alternation in party control of the chamber, thereby giving its forecasts greater political content. After the Reagan victory in 1980, the Republicans achieved a Senate majority. In subsequent elections, the central question then became whether they could keep it. In 1986, there was varied and vociferous opinion about whether the Republicans could hold on to the Senate (see the review in Lewis-Beck 1987). Using an earlier version of our model of Chapter 5, we issued a before-election 1986 forecast that the ruling Republicans would lose their majority. Such proved to be the case, for after the dust cleared the Democrats emerged with a 55-45 edge.

Our current Senate model has also been tried in the field. Before the 1990 contest, it forecasted a net Republican loss of 3 seats. This forecast ran heavily against the dominant view, that Republicans would certainly lose no seats (and might even pick up some). An important reason for this perspective is summed up by Thomas Mann (*Roll Call*, September 27, 1990, 26) of the Brookings Institution, who felt that the quality of Republican candidates would be telling: "The Republicans really do have the best challengers. Their success at candidate recruitment should turn into one or two more seats for the Republicans."

A Capitol Hill newspaper, *Roll Call*, canvassed numerous politicos, pundits, pollsters, and scholars (including us), asking them in September to forecast the 1990 contest. In Table 9.3 are listed eleven different Senate forecasts from this survey. Notice that none of them (save ours) called for a net Republican loss, which is what actually occurred. Further, our forecast of −3 for the Republicans was off by only 2 seats. Thus, we have some confidence in its 1992 performance.

Table 9.3 Before-the-Election Senate Forecasts, 1990

Observer	Predicted net Republican seat change
Republican Senate Campaign Committee	+5 to +2 seats
Norman Ornstein (American Enterprise Institute)	+3 to +1
Allan Lichtman and Ken DeCell (scholar and editor)	+2
Charles Cook (*Cook Political Report*)	+2
Stuart Rothenberg (*Political Report*)	+2
Thomas Mann (Brookings Institution)	+2 to +1
Eddie Mahe (GOP consultant)	+2 to +1
Linda Divall (*American Viewpoint*)	+1
John Gizzi (*Human Events*)	0
Democratic Senate Campaign Committee	0
Michael Lewis-Beck and Tom Rice	−3
Actual result	−1

Source: Roll Call, September 27, 1990, 1, 24, 26.

Note: After reviewing the forecasts, *Roll Call* made a forecast, calling the Senate exactly right at −1 for the Republicans.

Recall that the Senate forecasting model (equation 5.2) is based on five independent variables: income growth (E), presidential popularity (PP), midterm or not (M), seats exposed (X′), and party of the president (D). Here is the prediction equation:

$$SC = 2.17 + 1.44(E \times M) + 0.13PP - 0.84X' + 3.52D \quad \text{(Eq. 9.3)}$$

where SC = number of Senate seats gained or lost by the president's party; E = income growth from the fourth quarter of the year before the election to the second quarter of the election year; M = a dichotomous variable scored 0 for midterm elections, 1 for presidential elections; PP = percentage approving of how the president is handling his job in the June Gallup Poll; X′ = number of seats the president's party has up for reelection; D = a dichotomous variable for the president's party, scored 0 for Republican, 1 for Democrat.

As with the House model, the prediction equation for 1992 simplifies because we know scores on three of the variables: M = 1 (for a presidential election year); X′ = 13 (the number of seats the Republicans have up for reelection); D = 0 (a Republican president). When we plug these values into the prediction equation:

$$SC = 2.17 + 1.44(E \times 1) + 0.13PP - 0.84(13) + 3.52(0)$$

Table 9.4 Senate Election Forecasts (Change in Incumbent Seats, 1992), Under Different Popularity and Economic Conditions

$$SC = 2.17 + 1.44(E \times 1) + 0.13PP - 0.84(13) + 3.52(0)$$

	Presidential popularity (PP)		
Economic growth (E)	40%	50%	60%
−1%	−4.99	−3.69	−2.39
+1%	−2.11	−.81	.49
+2%	−.67	.63	1.93

Notes: Three variables for 1992 have known values, set at M = 1 (presidential election year); X′ = 13 (number of Republican seats up for reelection); D = 0 (a Republican president). The other two variables, PP (presidential popularity in the June 1992 Gallup Poll) and E (income growth rate from the fourth quarter of the year before the election to the second quarter of the election year), are presumed unknown. Therefore, each is set at three different possible scores, which are plugged into the prediction equation to generate the different forecasts.

Again, we observe that the remaining unknowns are income growth (E) and presidential popularity (PP). As with the presidency and the House, it is possible to deduce different forecast outcomes, depending on whether performance is good, average, or bad. In Table 9.4, different economic and popularity values are set (given the known values on M, X′, and D) and the different forecasts generated. Clearly, whether the Republicans are predicted to have a good or a bad year in the Senate depends considerably on the actual scores for the economy and popularity variables.

Conclusion

Election forecasters try to predict results before they happen. It is only through use that the scientific models of the political science forecaster can fulfill that purpose. To that end, we have laid bare the calculation rules of our models for elections to the presidency, the House, and the Senate. Under different election "scenarios," different 1992 outcomes can be calculated.

In Table 9.5, we summarize our forecasts, in terms of best case and worst case scenarios. Further, for completeness, the table adds forecasts for gubernatorial and state legislative races (from equations 7.2 and 7.4, respectively). Given the assumptions of these scenarios, Republican success in 1992 in all arenas depends heavily on the performance of the macroeconomy and the presidential administration in general. Perhaps

Table 9.5 Forecasts for Republicans in 1992, Best and Worst Case Scenarios

Electoral arena	Best case	Worst case
President (equation 3.5)	89.0% of the electoral vote	48.5% of the electoral vote
House (equation 4.5)	+4 seats	−35 seats
Senate (equation 5.2)	+2 seats	−5 seats
Governors (equation 7.2)	+1 seat	−6 seats
State legislatures (equation 7.4)	+1 legislature	−4 legislatures

Note: The best and worst case scenario forecasts are from Tables 9.1, 9.2, and 9.4, the lower right-hand and upper left-hand corners, respectively. The governor and state legislature scenarios use the indicated equations, making the same assumptions: best = +2 percent economic growth, 60 percent popularity; worst = −1 percent economic growth, 40 percent popularity.

this is as it should be. That is, the implication for voting behavior appears Jeffersonian: each citizen carefully weighs economic and noneconomic issues before deciding whether to cast out the incumbent party.

Through application of our models to upcoming contests, we are brought full circle in this study of elections. We began with the question, How should we forecast election outcomes? Our answer was that traditional methods—prognostication rules, tips from political insiders, informal observations of pundits, public opinion polls—were inadequate. Instead, we proposed the use of statistical models based on national economic and political measures. As we have now seen, these uncomplicated models forecast rather well. Why do they "work"? In a nutshell, because they are formulated from leading scientific explanations of how individual voters actually decide. While our macro-models obviously say nothing directly about individual behavior, these aggregate results are certainly compatible with a process many political scientists believe lies at the heart of democratic vote choice—reasonable evaluation of issues before selecting an alternative. Given this compatibility, we believe that future improvements in election forecasting will come increasingly from explorations and testing of voting theory.

APPENDIX

Election Forecasting Data

In this appendix are the data we used to develop our forecasting models. We include the data, along with auxiliary variables, in order that readers can build models themselves and easily update those models for forecasting future elections. As can be observed, the data sets are not large. Thus, they can readily be entered into a personal computer, and analyzed with any one of the several statistical packages that provide a regression routine. (Our models were run on MYSTAT.) The reader can replicate the final models in our text; respectively, equations 3.5, 4.3, 5.2, 7.2, 7.4, 8.5. The relevant variables for the models are labeled with the same letters as appear in the equations.

To locate new observations to add to the series, a few general tips may be useful. Most of the political variables can be found in the standard reference volumes of any library. Current scores, such as a recent election result or a new Gallup Poll, may first appear in newspapers, such as the *New York Times.* With regard to macroeconomic variables, current statistics are reported in considerable detail in the *Wall Street Journal.* At the end of 1991, the U.S. Department of Commerce began to emphasize the reporting of GDP (that is, GNP minus net income from overseas), to bring its economic measures more in accord with other industrial nations. Practically speaking, the use of GDP rather than GNP should make a negligible difference for election forecasting, since the two are almost perfectly correlated. Any serious search for hard-to-find variables may take you to the government documents section of your university library, or perhaps to the business school library. In certain instances, you might want to go directly to the source, which we identify. (The French case has its own complications, which we will address.)

Table A.1 Presidential Model

	Variables				
Year	(1) Incumbent share, Electoral College (V)	(2) GNP change (G)	(3) Presidential popularity (PP)	(4) House incumbent party loss (HS)	(5) Primary score (%) (C)
1948	57.1%	2.42%	39	−54	1 (63.9)
1952	16.8	0.07	32	−29	0 (1.6)
1956	86.1	0.26	69	−18	1 (85.9)
1960	40.8	1.42	49	−47	1 (89.9)
1964	90.3	3.11	74	−5	0 (17.7)
1968	35.5	2.88	40	−48	0 (2.2)
1972	96.7	4.18	56	−12	1 (86.9)
1976	44.6	2.33	45	−48	0 (53.3)
1980	9.1	−1.38	21	−16	0 (51.2)
1984	97.6	3.95	52	−27	1 (98.6)
1988	79.2	1.91	51	−5	1 (68.0)

Sources: The Electoral College vote is available in many reference volumes, including almanacs and encyclopedias; see, in particular, the *Statistical Abstract of the United States.* The GNP figures used to calculate the percentage change scores are prepared by the U.S. Department of Commerce. Quarterly GNP figures in constant dollars are available in the Department of Commerce publication *Survey of Current Business.* A preliminary second quarter figure, needed to calculate the change, is usually available by May. The final figure is available by July. The presidential popularity data are from the Gallup Poll. When two or more polls are conducted in July, the first poll is used. Popularity figures can be obtained by contacting Gallup Poll directly or by consulting *Gallup Reports.* The results are also widely reported in the press. The figures reported in column 3 are the percentage of respondents who reported they approved of the job the president was doing. The data for House seats are widely available; we collected the data from various volumes of the *Statistical Abstract of the United States.* The data for primaries are often available in the popular press during a campaign; a particularly reliable source is *Congressional Quarterly Weekly Report.*

Notes: The dependent variable is (column 1) V = incumbent party percentage of the Electoral College vote. Independent variables are: (column 2) G = percentage change (nonannualized) in GNP (constant dollars) from the fourth quarter of the year before the election to the second quarter of the election year; (column 3) PP = presidential popularity in July before the election; (column 4) HS = incumbent party seat loss in U.S. House in the previous midterm election; (column 5) C = percentage of the total primary vote the incumbent party nominee receives, scored 1 if the nominee wins at least 60 percent of the vote and 0 if the nominee wins less than 60 percent (the figures in parentheses are the actual primary vote percentages for the incumbent party candidates).

Table A.2 Dependent Variables: Senate, House, Gubernatorial, and State Legislative Models

	Variables			
Year	(1) Senate incumbent party change (SC)	(2) House incumbent party change (HC)	(3) Governorships incumbent party change (GC)	(4) State legislature partisan change (SL)
1948	9	75	7	2
1950	−5	−29	−7	0
1952	−2	−23	−5	−3
1954	−1	−18	−9	−6
1956	0	−3	−1	−2
1958	−13	−47	−6	−11
1960	1	21	2	8
1962	2	−5	0	−3
1964	1	37	−1	9
1966	−4	−48	−8	−9
1968	−7	−4	−6	−4
1970	1	−12	−10	−2
1972	−2	12	−2	−1
1974	−5	−48	−6	−12
1976	1	−1	−1	0
1978	−3	−16	−5	−4
1980	−12	−33	−5	−2
1982	1	−27	−8	−4
1984	−1	17	1	0
1986	−8	−5	8	−2
1988	0	−2	−2	−2
1990	−1	−8	−1	−3

Source: Statistical Abstract of the United States, various volumes.

Note: The dependent variables are: (column 1) SC = incumbent party seat loss/gain in U.S. Senate elections; (column 2) HC = incumbent party seat loss/gain in U.S. House elections; (column 3) GC = governorships lost/gained by the incumbent party; (column 4) SL = change in partisan control of state legislatures for the incumbent party (for control the incumbent party must control both chambers).

Table A.3 Independent Variables: Income

Year	(1) Income 4th-2d (E)	(2) Income 1st-2d	(3) Income 2d-2d	(4) E × M
1948	5.46%	2.94%	6.62%	5.46%
1950	6.67	−0.51	7.21	0
1952	0.87	0.95	1.79	0.87
1954	−0.40	−0.49	−0.18	0
1956	1.60	0.75	5.22	1.60
1958	0.08	0.74	0.48	0
1960	1.65	0.58	2.02	1.65
1962	1.83	0.81	4.48	0
1964	4.74	2.71	7.47	4.74
1966	1.17	0.57	5.61	0
1968	2.91	1.58	4.49	2.91
1970	2.18	1.72	5.14	0
1972	1.61	0.95	2.06	1.61
1974	−2.77	−1.00	−1.01	0
1976	2.03	0.49	1.38	2.03
1978	2.85	1.62	5.52	0
1980	−1.26	−1.79	−0.09	−1.26
1982	0.32	0.68	1.16	0
1984	2.67	0.40	6.30	2.67
1986	3.35	1.51	3.32	0
1988	1.73	0.58	5.35	1.73
1990	0.68	0.07	1.68	0

Source: U.S. Department of Commerce, *Survey of Current Business.*

Notes: Variables are percentage change in real disposable personal income (constant dollars) from the fourth quarter of the year before the election to the second quarter of the election year (column 1); from the first quarter of the election year to the second quarter of the election year (column 2); and from the second quarter of the year before the election to the second quarter of the election year (column 3). Column 4 is column 1 (E) multiplied by the midterm measure (M—scored 0 for midterm years, 1 for presidential years).

Table A.4 Independent Variables: GNP

	Variables		
Year	(1) GNP 4th-2d	(2) GNP 1st-2d	(3) GNP 2d-2d
1948	2.42%	1.78%	4.03%
1950	7.04	2.86	6.79
1952	0.07	−0.24	3.45
1954	−1.78	−0.40	−3.02
1956	0.26	0.46	2.48
1958	−1.50	0.54	−2.46
1960	1.42	−0.29	1.82
1962	2.36	1.04	6.16
1964	3.11	0.86	5.67
1966	2.23	0.26	6.26
1968	2.88	1.70	4.95
1970	−0.70	−0.09	−0.55
1972	4.18	1.94	4.71
1974	−0.28	0.28	0.52
1976	2.33	0.45	5.52
1978	4.07	3.16	5.89
1980	−1.38	−2.36	−0.68
1982	−1.21	0.30	−2.16
1984	3.95	1.34	7.36
1986	1.15	−0.44	2.93
1988	1.91	0.90	4.90
1990	0.53	0.11	1.04

Source: U.S. Department of Commerce, *Survey of Current Business.*

Notes: Variables are percentage change (nonannualized) in GNP (constant dollars) from the fourth quarter of the year before the election to the second quarter of the election year (column 1); from the first quarter of the election year to the second quarter of the election year (column 2); and from the second quarter of the year before the election to the second quarter of the election year (column 3).

Table A.5 Independent Variables: Presidential Popularity (PP)

	Variables[a]	
Year	(1) July	(2) June
1948	39%	39%
1950	37	46
1952	32	32
1954	62	75
1956	69	69
1958	54	52
1960	61	49
1962	71	66
1964	74	74
1966	48	56
1968	40	40
1970	55	61
1972	56	56
1974	26	24
1976	45	45
1978	42	39
1980	31	21
1982	45	45
1984	52	52
1986	61	63
1988	51	51
1990	67	63

Sources: Gallup Reports, various issues.

[a]Presidential popularity as measured in July and June before the election.

Table A.6 Independent Variables: Exposure

	Variables		
Year	(1) House (X)	(2) Senate (X′)	(3) Governorships (XR)
1948	−69	14	4
1950	6	21	−2
1952	−23	14	−3
1954	44	13	−12
1956	26	17	2
1958	23	21	9
1960	−24	11	8
1962	6	19	−9
1964	1	25	−12
1966	38	19	−7
1968	−10	23	−8
1970	15	8	−13
1972	3	19	5
1974	15	15	9
1976	−33	11	5
1978	35	16	−17
1980	19	24	−9
1982	15	12	3
1984	−12	19	1
1986	5	22	20
1988	0	14	−1
1990	−2	17	−2

Sources: (Column 1) *Statistical Abstract of the United States;* (columns 2 and 3) *Congressional Quarterly Weekly Report.* Other news sources may be used as well.

Notes: (Column 1) X = number of seats the incumbent party has exposed in the U.S. House (for an explanation of how House exposure is calculated, see Table 4.4); (column 2) X′ = number of seats the incumbent party has up for reelection in the U.S. Senate (for an explanation of how Senate exposure is calculated, see the discussion in Chapter 5); (column 3) XR = number of incumbent party governorships at stake relative to the number of out-party governorships at stake (for an explanation of how gubernatorial exposure is calculated, see the discussion in Chapter 7).

Table A.7 Independent Variables: Trends and Terms

	Variables				
Year	(1) Election type (M)	(2) President's party (D)	(3) Time in White House (T)	(4) Governor's term (GT)	(5) Legislative redistricting (B)
1948	1	1	4	0	0
1950	0	1	4	0	1
1952	1	1	4	0	0
1954	0	0	1	0	0
1956	1	0	2	0	0
1958	0	0	3	0	0
1960	1	0	4	0	1
1962	0	1	1	0	0
1964	1	1	2	0	0
1966	0	1	3	0	0
1968	1	1	4	0	0
1970	0	0	1	0	1
1972	1	0	2	0	0
1974	0	0	3	0	0
1976	1	0	4	1	0
1978	0	1	1	1	0
1980	1	1	2	1	1
1982	0	0	1	1	0
1984	1	0	2	1	0
1986	0	0	3	1	0
1988	1	0	4	1	0
1990	0	0	4	1	1

Notes: (Column 1) M = type of election, scored 0 for midterm years and 1 for presidential years; (column 2) D = party of the president, scored 0 for Republican and 1 for Democratic; (column 3) T = time in the White House, scored 1 for first midterm election after a change in party control of the presidency, 2 for the year of a party's first reelection, 3 for the party's second midterm election—that is, after a party has won the presidency for the second time, and 4 for all other elections; (column 4) GT = gubernatorial length of term variable, scored 0 for elections from 1948 to 1972 and 1 for elections after 1974; and (column 5) B = state legislative redistricting variable, scored 0 for all years except 1950, 1960, 1970, 1980, 1990, which are scored 1.

The French Model

The data set for our final national French election model, which combines presidential and National Assembly elections, is provided in Table A.8. French data are harder to locate, at least on this side of the Atlantic, than are the American forecasting data. Basically, if you know the party of the president, you need only locate the two key measures: popularity and economic growth.

Many presidential popularity figures are reported in the French press. Our model employs the IFOP (*Institut Français d' Opinion Publique*) presidential "satisfaction" measure, now regularly reported in the newspaper *Journal du Dimanche,* which may well be available in your university library. Also, other French newspapers will report it, but perhaps not regularly. *Le Monde* is always a good first place to look for this IFOP popularity figure, which continues the longest running popularity series available in France. Another big polling organization is SOFRES, which regularly asks about "confidence" in the president. These monthly results are published in *Figaro* and give estimates similar to those of IFOP.

With regard to the quarterly GDP growth rate from six months before, the reader should also search the French press, especially *Le Monde.* It, as well as other leading French newspapers, reports on current economic conditions, as measured by the national government economic and social data-gathering organization, INSEE. That organization publishes current bulletins, which are difficult to come by outside France. For a good English language source, try the *Economist* magazine. At the back of every issue, current estimates of economic conditions for France, as well as other Western countries, are provided.

Table A.8 Variables for the French Model

	Variables			
Year (election)	(1) Opposition's vote (O)	(2) Popularity (FP)	(3) GDP change (FG)	(4) President's party (PL)
1958 (A)	43.4%	67	0.73	0
1962 (A)	44.2	61	1.67	0
1965 (P)	45.5	58	1.90	0
1967 (A)	45.0	64	1.08	0
1968 (A)	41.0	53	0.96	0
1969 (P)	42.5	58	1.60	0
1973 (A)	46.4	54	1.10	0
1974 (P)	49.4	57	1.40	0
1978 (A)	49.5	49	0.74	0
1981 (P)	51.8	44	0.00	0
1981 (A)	55.7	37	−0.25	0
1986 (A)	56.0	34	0.30	1
1988 (P)	46.0	56	1.50	1
1988 (A)	50.3	60	1.50	1

Sources: The presidential voting data are from *Le Monde: Dossiers et Documents,* various issues. The legislative voting data are from the following: Jacques Chapsal, *La Vie Politique en France depuis 1940,* 3d ed. (Paris: Presses Universitaires de France, 1972), 657-664; Jacques Chapsal and Alain Lancelot, *La Vie Politique en France depuis 1940,* 4th ed. (Paris: Presses Universitaires de France, 1975), 663-664; *Sondages* 40 (1978): 8; David S. Bell, ed., *Contemporary French Political Parties* (London: Croom Helm, 1982), 190; *Le Monde: Dossiers et Documents,* special legislative election issues for 1986 and 1988. The poll data are from IFOP (*Institut Français d' Opinion Publique*) polls. GDP figures are from various issues of *Main Economic Indicators,* OECD.

Notes: A = National Assembly elections, P = presidential elections. The dependent variable is (column 1) O = opposition vote percentage against the president or the president's party coalition. Independent variables are: (column 2) FP = presidential popularity six months before the election; (column 3) FG = annual growth rate for real GDP in the quarter occurring six months before the election; (column 4) L = party of the president, scored 1 if the president is from a left-wing party and 0 otherwise.

REFERENCES

Abraham, Bovas, and Johannes Ledolter. 1983. *Statistical Methods for Forecasting.* New York: Wiley.

Abramowitz, Alan L. 1988. "An Improved Model for Predicting Presidential Election Outcomes." *PS* 21: 843-847.

Abramowitz, Alan L., and Jeffrey A. Sigel. 1986. "Determinants of the Outcomes of U.S. Senate Elections." *Journal of Politics* 48: 433-439.

Achen, Christopher H. 1990. "What Does 'Explained Variance' Explain?" *Political Analysis* 2: 173-184.

Asher, Herbert B. 1988. *Presidential Elections and American Politics.* Chicago: Dorsey.

Bean, Louis H. 1972. *How to Predict the 1972 Election.* New York: Quadrangle Books.

Berry, William, and Stanley Feldman. 1985. *Multiple Regression in Practice.* Newbury Park, Calif.: Sage.

Bibby, 1983. "Patterns in Midterm Gubernatorial and State Legislative Elections." *Public Opinion* 6: 41-46.

Blake, Debbie. 1991. "Stock Traders Put Their Money Where the Votes Are." *Spectator* 24 (2): 4.

Brody, Richard, and Lee Sigelman. 1983. "Presidential Popularity and Presidential Elections: An Update and Extension." *Public Opinion Quarterly* 47: 325-328.

Broh, C. Anthony. 1980. "Whether Bellwethers or Weather-Jars Indicate Election Outcomes." *Western Political Quarterly* 33: 564-570.

Buchanan, William. 1986. "Election Predictions: An Empirical Assessment." *Public Opinion Quarterly* 50: 222-227.

Campbell, Angus. 1964. "Voters and Elections: Past and Present." *Journal of Politics* 26: 745-757.

___. 1966. "Interpreting the Presidential Victory." In *The National Election of 1964,* ed. Milton C. Cummings, Jr. Washington, D.C.: Brookings.

Campbell, Angus, Philip E. Converse, Warren E. Miller, and Donald E. Stokes. 1960. *The American Voter.* New York: Wiley.

Campbell, James E. 1985. "Explaining Presidential Losses in Midterm Congressional Elections." *Journal of Politics* 47: 1140-1157.

___. 1986a. "Forecasting the 1986 Midterm Elections to the House of Representatives." *PS* (Winter): 83-87.

———. 1986b. "Predicting Seat Gains from Presidential Coattails." *American Journal of Political Science* 30: 165-183.

———. 1986c. "Presidential Coattails and Midterm Losses in State Legislative Elections." *American Political Science Review* 80: 45-63.

———. 1987. "The Revised Theory of Surge and Decline." *American Journal of Political Science* 31: 965-979. .

Campbell, James E., and Kenneth A. Wink. 1990. "Trial-Heat Forecasts of the Presidential Vote." *American Politics Quarterly* 18: 251-269.

Chubb, John E. 1988. "Institutions, the Economy, and the Dynamics of State Elections." *American Political Science Review* 82: 133-154.

Converse, Philip E., Angus Campbell, Warren E. Miller, and Donald E. Stokes. 1966. *Elections and the Political Order.* New York: Wiley.

Converse, Philip E., Warren E. Miller, Jerrold G. Rusk, and Arthur C. Wolfe. 1969. "Continuity and Change in American Politics: Parties and Issues in the 1968 Election." *American Political Science Review* 63: 1083-1105.

Crespi, Irving. 1988. *Pre-Election Polling: Sources of Accuracy and Error.* New York: Russell Sage.

Diaconis, Peter, and Fred Mosteller. 1989. "Methods for Studying Coincidences." *Journal of the American Statistical Association* 84: 853-861.

Dye, Thomas R. 1984. "Party and Policy in the States." *Journal of Politics* 46: 1097-1116.

Erbring, Lutz. 1989. "Individuals Writ Large: An Epilogue on the Ecological Fallacy." *Political Analysis* 1: 235-270.

Erikson, Robert S. 1989. "Economic Conditions and the Presidential Vote." *American Political Science Review* 83: 567-573.

———. 1990. "Economic Conditions and the Congressional Vote: A Review of the Macro Level Evidence." *American Journal of Political Science* 34: 373-399.

Erikson, Robert S., Gerald C. Wright, Jr., and John P. McIver. 1989. "Political Parties, Public Opinion, and State Policy in the United States." *American Political Science Review* 83: 729-750.

Fair, Ray C. 1978. "The Effect of Economic Events on Votes for President." *Review of Economics and Statistics* 60: 159-172.

———. 1982. "The Effect of Economic Events on Votes for President: 1980 Results." *Review of Economics and Statistics* 64: 322-325.

———. 1988. "The Effect of Economic Events on Votes for President: 1984 Update." *Political Behavior* 10: 168-179.

Fiorina, Morris P. 1981. *Retrospective Voting in American National Elections.* New Haven: Yale University Press.

Forsythe, Robert, Forrest Nelson, George Neumann, and John Wright. 1989. "The Iowa Presidential Stock Market: A Field Experiment." In *Research in Experimental Economics,* vol. 4, ed. R. M. Issac. Westport, Conn.: JAI Press.

Fox, John. 1991. *Regression Diagnostics.* Newbury Park, Calif.: Sage.

Frankovic, Kathleen A. 1985. "The 1984 Election: The Irrelevance of the Campaign." *PS* 18: 39-47.

———. 1990. "Media Polls: Monitoring Changes in Public Opinion." *ICPSR Bulletin* (February): 1-3.

Hibbing, John R., and John R. Alford. 1982. "Economic Conditions and the Forgotten Side of Congress: A Foray into U.S. Senate Elections." *British Journal of Political Science* 12: 505-513.

Hibbs, Douglas A. 1982. "President Reagan's Mandate from the 1980 Elections: A Shift to the Right?" *American Politics Quarterly* 10: 387-420.

___. 1987. *The American Political Economy.* Cambridge: Harvard University Press.

Hibbs, Douglas A., and Nicholas Vasilatos. 1981. "Economics and Politics in France: Economic Performance and Political Support for Presidents Pompidou and Giscard d'Estaing." *European Journal of Political Research* 9: 133-145.

Jacobson, Gary C. 1981. "Strategic Politicians and Congressional Elections, 1946-1980. Paper delivered at the annual meeting of the American Political Science Association, New York, September 3-6.

___. 1983. *The Politics of Congressional Elections.* Boston: Little, Brown.

___. 1987. *The Politics of Congressional Elections,* 2d ed. Boston: Little, Brown.

___. 1989. "Strategic Politicians and the Dynamics of U.S. House Elections, 1946-1986. *American Political Science Review* 83: 773-793.

___. 1990. "Does the Economy Matter in Midterm Elections?" *American Journal of Political Science* 34: 400-404.

Jacobson, Gary C., and Samuel Kernell. 1983. *Strategy and Choice in Congressional Elections.* New Haven: Yale University Press.

Jewell, Malcolm, 1968. "State Decision-Making: The Governor Revisited." In *American Governmental Institutions,* ed. Aaron Wildavsky and Nelson Polsby. Chicago: Rand McNally.

Jung, C. G. 1955. *Synchronicity: An Acausal Connecting Principle.* New York: Pantheon Books.

Kalton, Graham. 1983. *Introduction to Survey Sampling.* Beverly Hills, Calif.: Sage.

Kelejian, H. H., and W. E. Oates. 1974. *Introduction to Econometrics: Principles and Applications.* New York: Harper and Row.

Kenski, Henry C., and Edward C. Dreyer. 1977. "In Search of State Presidential Bellwethers." *Social Science Quarterly* 58: 498-505.

Kernell, Samuel. 1977. "Presidential Popularity and Negative Voting." *American Political Science Review* 71: 44-66.

Key, V. O., Jr. 1949. *Southern Politics.* New York: Knopf.

Kiewiet, D. Roderick. 1983. *Macroeconomics and Micropolitics: The Electoral Effects of Economic Issues.* Chicago: University of Chicago Press.

Kiewiet, D. Roderick, and Douglas Rivers. 1985. "A Retrospective on Retrospective Voting." In *Economic Conditions and Electoral Outcomes: The United States and Western Europe,* ed. Heinz Eulau and Michael S. Lewis-Beck, 207-231. New York: Agathon Books.

King, Gary. 1990a. "On Political Methodology." *Political Analysis* 2: 1-30.

___. 1990b. "Stochastic Variation: A Comment on Lewis-Beck and Skalaban's 'The R-Squared.'" *Political Analysis* 2: 185-200.

Koestler, Arthur. 1971. *The Case of the Midwife Toad.* New York: Vintage.

Kramer, Gerald H. 1971. "Short-Term Fluctuations in U.S. Voting Behavior." *American Political Science Review* 65: 131-143.

———. 1983. "Ecological Fallacy Revisited: Aggregate- versus Individual-Level Findings on Economics and Elections, and Sociotropic Voting." *American Political Science Review* 77: 92-111.

Lafay, Jean-Dominique. 1985. "Political Change and Stability of the Popularity Function: The French General Election of 1981." In *Economic Conditions and Electoral Outcomes: The United States and Western Europe,* ed. Heinz Eulau and Michael S. Lewis-Beck, 78-97. New York: Agathon Books.

Lewis-Beck, Michael S. 1980a. *Applied Regression: An Introduction.* Beverly Hills, Calif.: Sage.

———. 1980b. "Economic Conditions and Executive Popularity: The French Experience." *American Journal of Political Science* 24: 306-324.

———. 1983. "Economics and the French Voter: A Microanalysis." *Public Opinion Quarterly* 47: 347-360.

———. 1984. "France: The Stalled Electorate." In *Electoral Change in Advanced Industrial Societies: Realignment or Dealignment?* ed. Russell J. Dalton, Scott Flanagan, and Paul Allen Beck, 425-448. Princeton, N.J.: Princeton University Press.

———. 1985. "Election Forecasts in 1984: How Accurate Were They?" *PS* 18: 53-62.

———. 1987. "A Model Performance." *Public Opinion* 9: 57-58.

———. 1988. *Economics and Elections: The Major Western Democracies.* Ann Arbor: University of Michigan Press.

Lewis-Beck, Michael S., and Tom W. Rice. 1983. "Localism in Presidential Elections: The Home State Advantage." *American Journal of Political Science* 27: 548-556.

———. 1984. "Forecasting U.S. House Elections." *Legislative Studies Quarterly* 9: 475-486.

Lewis-Beck, Michael S., and Andrew Skalaban. 1990. "The R-Squared: Some Straight Talk." *Political Analysis* 2: 153-172.

———. In press. 1992. "The French Electorate: From Change to Change?" In *Electoral Change: Responses to Evolving Social and Attitudinal Structures in Fifteen Countries,* ed. Mark Franklin, Thomas Mackie, and Henry Valen. Cambridge: Cambridge University Press.

Lewis-Beck, Michael S., and Peverill Squire. 1990. "The Transformation of the American State: The New Era-New Deal Transition." *Journal of Politics* 53: 106-121.

Lipset, Seymour. 1985. "The Elections, the Economy, and Public Opinion." *PS* 18: 28-38.

Mackuen, Michael B. 1983. "Political Drama, Economic Conditions, and the Dynamics of Presidential Popularity." *American Journal of Political Science* 27: 165-192.

Mackuen, Michael B., Robert Erikson, and James Stimson. 1989. "Macropartisanship." *American Political Science Review* 82: 125-142.

Mann, Thomas E. 1978. *Unsafe at Any Margin: Interpreting Congressional Elections.* Washington, D.C.: American Enterprise Institute.

Mann, Thomas E., and Norman J. Ornstein. 1984. "Congressional Elections: What's Ahead." *Public Opinion* (June/July): 43-46.

Markus, Gregory. 1988. "The Impact of Personal and National Economic Conditions on the Presidential Vote: A Pooled Cross-Sectional Analysis." *American Journal of Political Science* 32: 137-154.

Marra, Robin F., and Charles W. Ostrom, Jr. 1989. "Explaining Seat Change in the U.S. House of Representatives, 1950-1986." *American Journal of Political Science* 33: 541-569.

Mueller, John E. 1973. *War, Presidents and Public Opinion.* New York: Wiley.

Norpoth, Helmut. 1985. "The Economy and Presidential Popularity in the United States." Paper presented at the Thirteenth World Congress of the International Political Science Association, Paris, July 15-20.

Norpoth, Helmut, Michael S. Lewis-Beck, and Jean-Dominique Lafay, eds. 1991. *Economics and Politics: The Calculus of Support.* Ann Arbor: University of Michigan Press.

Oppenheimer, Bruce I, James A. Stimson, and Richard W. Waterman. 1986. "Interpreting U.S. Congressional Elections: The Exposure Thesis." *Legislative Studies Quarterly* 11: 227-247.

Ostrom, Charles W., and Dennis M. Simon. 1985. "The Man in the Teflon Suit? The Environmental Connection, Political Drama, and Popular Support in the Reagan Presidency." *Public Opinion Quarterly* 53: 353-387.

Paldam, Martin. 1986. "The Distribution of Election Results and the Two Explanations of the Cost of Ruling." *European Journal of Political Economy* 2: 5-24.

——. 1991. "How Robust Is the Vote Function? A Study of Seventeen Nations over Four Decades." In *Economics and Politics: The Calculus of Support,* ed. Helmut Norpoth, Michael S. Lewis-Beck, and Jean-Dominique Lafay, 9-32. Ann Arbor: University of Michigan Press.

Peltzman, Samuel. 1987. "Economic Conditions and Gubernatorial Elections." *AEA Papers and Proceedings* 7: 293-297.

Pindyck, Robert S., and Daniel Rubinfeld. 1990. *Econometric Models and Economic Forecasts,* 3d ed. New York: McGraw-Hill.

Polsby, Nelson W., and Aaron Wildavsky. 1984. *Presidential Elections: Strategies of American Electoral Politics.* New York: Scribner.

Pomper, Gerald M., ed. 1989. *The Election of 1988.* Chatham, N.J.: Chatham House.

Roll, Charles W., Jr. "Straws in the Wind: The Record of the *Daily News* Poll." *Public Opinion Quarterly* 32: 251-266.

Rosenstone, Steven J. 1983. *Forecasting Presidential Elections.* New Haven: Yale University Press.

Sabato, Larry. 1983. *Goodbye to Good-time Charlie.* Washington, D.C.: CQ Press.

Safran, William. 1991. *The French Polity.* New York: Longman.

Squire, Peverill. 1988. "Why the 1936 *Literary Digest* Poll Failed." *Public Opinion Quarterly* 52: 125-133.

Stein, Robert. 1990. "Economic Voting for Governor and U.S. Senator: The Electoral Consequences of Federalism." *Journal of Politics* 52: 29-53.

Tufte, Edward R. 1974. *Data Analysis for Politics and Policy.* Englewood Cliffs, N.J.: Prentice-Hall.

——. 1975. "Determinants of the Outcomes of Midterm Congressional Elections." *American Political Science Review* 69: 812-826.

———. 1978. *Political Control of the Economy*. Princeton, N.J.: Princeton University Press.

Wattenberg, Martin. 1991. *The Rise of Candidate-Centered Politics: Presidential Elections in the 1980s*. Cambridge: Harvard University Press.

Weisberg, Herbert F., and Bruce D. Bowen. 1977. *An Introduction to Survey Research and Data Analysis*. San Francisco: W. H. Freeman.

INDEX